# Individuality and Encounter

## A BRIEF JOURNEY INTO LONELINESS AND SENSITIVITY GROUPS

### Clark Moustakas

THE MERRILL-PALMER INSTITUTE
DETROIT, MICHIGAN

HOWARD A. DOYLE PUBLISHING COMPANY
Cambridge, Massachusetts 02139

INDIVIDUALITY AND ENCOUNTER

*Library of Congress Catalog Card Number 68-25353*

Third Printing  1971

For Kerry

with whom my awareness of creative
loneliness began and continues

# Contents

# Foreword

This book conveys a spirit that requires that I express my own individuality by revealing my being. You are unique and will have your own experience with this book no matter what I say about it. So let me begin from where I am in regard to loneliness, solitude, and encounter. A great deal can be written, but here is what emerges from my memory in the finite amount of time that I have to write this foreword.

Not too long ago I wrote to Clark Moustakas about an intense period of suffering that came from my experience with loneliness and alienation. I wrote:

> The moments of suffering and loneliness are over for now. I was able to stay with the experience by telling myself that to live fully I must be willing to experience the pain of life—the loneliness of being away from loved friends, the accumulated pain of seeing the denying faces, the masks and games people present to you as their selves. I could not emerge from the pain by myself. My heart needed contact with a loved friend. Then long walks where I found myself smiling in front of laughing, beautiful children. The joy of tender faces. Even the leaves blowing on the ground seemed to be waving hello. The heart responds in funny ways—the moments of suffering were over.
>
> I did not try to give order to the experience or come to terms with it intellectually. My heart led the way. Thus the change in feeling was a change in my being— not in the "intellectual" knowledge of me or the superficial ordering of my life that would deny my being. Now I can again feel the sweetness of life. I am free to be— to experience love, joy, pain, and sorrow. I am willing to face the blood, cries, and tears along with the joys of life. I am willing to be!

I still felt alone when my suffering ceased though I felt in harmony with myself and nature. Moments of solitude emerged that were beautiful because I stayed with the experience of loneliness. My aloneness took on a different quality.

Months later I found myself reflecting on the above experience. At that time "thinking about" my experience did not seem superficial or denying of my being. The thinking was not planned but emerged and seemed existentially valid. I began to reflect on what caused me pain or joy. I started to write.

> There was a time when necessities came in shapes and sizes
> When the core of meaning was actually the shell of life
> But that was before I became myself
> Though what I am and become is as ephemeral as a day's wind
> It is me and I will be.
> I have no need for the Emperor's clothes
> That hide you from all but the innocent
> What I seek is to have meaning and to be meaningful
> To love and to receive love
> To have meaning I must be true to myself
> To be meaningful I must be responded to as I am
> I want to live authentically and spontaneously
> My masks are gone and I am struggling to be
> I face the void with the pains of birth
> And need Love to nourish me into being.

Again intense suffering. Here I was a psychologist at a mental hospital. I had struggled to get there. But this nine to five world was alien. I was listening to the timeless sound of my heart and feeling the pain of seeing children diagnosed, classified, medicated but denied. Staff meetings were rigid, with each "discipline" presenting their professional opinions and fragmenting a human being until he was nothing but a label. If we could only forget our roles and be silent. The child can speak for himself. I wanted authentic feelings from the staff, a sense of who I was dealing with. Fortunately the "disturbed" children were real and responded with honesty.  Confrontations and encounters with staff members began to come and are still coming. . . .

My need for meaningful encounters with people became more acute, especially with those I loved.  I sought a response from a woman I loved and writing emerged.

> Let us communicate in the language of being
> Touching, feeling, sensing
> I have no need to define or classify you
> Or "know about" you
> My heart reveals in silence that you are beautiful
> And that is good
> I want to meet with you in a spirit beyond possession
> A spirit that allows us to be what we must
> With freedom to flow together or to be Alone
> I want to transcend time and space
> And affirm our ephemeral beings
> With the eternal value of Love.

Man's task is to find the way to himself.  We must also be open to receive the other, to help him to become, to seek revelation and transformation into greater authenticity and being.  Remove the masks.  Let us cut the rope that binds us to the arbitrary and listen to the sounds of our hearts.  Let the heart speak to others, through encounters and confrontations, by words or in silence.  Being present to the experience of one's self and the other is man's way of affirming Life.

Charles Marcantonio
Pontiac State Hospital
Pontiac, Michigan

# Preface

The experiences of *Individuality and Encounter* grew out of deep personal struggles, searching self-denial and self-transcendence, hours and hours of lonely self-reflection, encounters of absolute pain and prolonged anguish, many, many gentle, tender, beautiful moments of dialogue and silence, and moments of sharing and of love with other persons. In so many ways I have lived in the deeper regions of myself and in profound resonance with others. I have reached timeless, enduring relationships and I have faced the temporary, shattering effects of hypocrisy and betrayal. I have gone out, beyond what I have known, in doubt, in uncertainty, in shock; I have faced the extremes of feelings in anger, in joy, in suffering, in passion. I have wept with others in long hours of agony, and the tears have dissipated into laughter and I have laughed with others into tears of ecstasy. Sometimes I have felt that I could not go on living so intensely, so absolutely, so fully, moment by moment, and I have withdrawn into meditation and into loneliness. But each time I have returned, ready to enter into life, ready to experience its potential—alone, in person-to-person encounters, in groups. In so many ways, while maintaining my own identity, I have changed my style of living and my presence with others in family experiences, in friendships, in therapy, in teaching. I am constantly startled by the unexplored ranges of myself and the untapped potentials in human relations. At last, I believe I am learning to face directly and openly human possibilities for awareness and for truth, for love and for companionship; I am increasingly recognizing human capacities for living authentically and for drawing from life increasing value, meaning, and depth.

For these many transformations and for the affirmation of the enduring nature of my being, for the recognition and the welcome, for the gentle, tender facilitating of my development as a person, and for the hard, harsh and even hostile criticisms and attacks, which, at times, rendered me immobile and numb but which ultimately contributed to my personal growth, I thank many persons. First of all, I express my appreciation to all the groups (of course, this means each person in these groups)—sensory awareness, basic encounter, marathon, experiences of intensive human life in the extremes and in the quietness of silence, loneliness, and meditation. These awakenings, awarenesses, and meanings have been facilitated by my classes at The Merrill-Palmer Institute, by my workshops at Esalen Institute in Big Sur, California, and by my intensive group meetings with students and faculty in counseling and guidance, particularly at the University of Florida, Northern Illinois University, Arizona State University, Purdue University, Iowa State College, the University of Rochester, and Michigan State University, and also at the following universities and institutes, in departments of psychology, education, and family life, and in colleges of liberal arts: Pacific Oaks College, New Horizons in Los Gatos, California, San Jose State College, North Carolina Learning Institute, and the University of Connecticut. I also express my appreciation to the Association of Humanistic Psychology for creating and sponsoring annually experiences that tap human potential, generate real life, and enable persons to encounter one another and begin I-Thou relationships. I wish to thank the individuals who helped create the groups and who were willing to face the challenges and risks of honesty and intimacy in human relations, including Michael Murphy and Hobart Thomas, Esalen Institute; Ted Landsman, University of Florida; Betty Bosdell, Northern Illinois University; Bob Frank, Iowa State College; Harold Munson, University of Rochester; Pat McGreevy, Arizona State University; Cereta Perry and Norm Story, Michigan State University; Richard Nelson, Purdue University; Mary Pieters,

Pacific Oaks College; Lee Swenson and Glennys Spitze, New Horizons and San Jose State College; Stanley Bean, North Carolina Learning Institute; Eleanore Luckey, University of Connecticut; and Pauline Knapp and William Rioux of The Merrill-Palmer Institute.

I wish to recognize a number of other individuals who are within this book, particularly Charles Marcantonio, Tee Herrington, Donna Turley, Margarethe Wiest, and Mavis Wolfe. Finally, I express my appreciation to Bob, Wendy, Kerry, Steve, Beth, and my wife, Betty, who at times shared the pain and struggle and who at times were swept into the extremes of life and caught up in the explosive encounters, in the search to differentiate the real from the phony, and in the journey to discover meaning, beauty, and love.

Clark Moustakas
Detroit, Michigan
March 17, 1968

# CHAPTER 1

# Individuality
# and
# Identity

As I struggle with this theme, the individual in mass society, I am faced with an immediate challenge. How can I remain an individual right now, at this moment, and come through as an individual, rather than become a lecturer and carry out the role of an observer of the human scene? Can this structure, which in itself is impersonal, be transcended? Obviously, there is a difference between writing a skillful lecture on individuality and being an individual, a difference between talking about reality and being real. The most rigid conformist can write a brilliant essay on uniqueness and individuality. It is easy to slip into roles, to act out labels, to play games, and to remain comfortably anonymous. It is much more difficult to make individuality a living reality and not a series of dead abstractions or narcissistic forms.

Remaining an individual in the face of mass movements and social pressures is a basic problem of man today. We are pushed to conform on every side, in the places where we spend most of the hours of the day. Right now, in this situation, we are faced wth a dilemma, that of transcending the purely academic culture, that of breaking through the system of rules that define appropriate behavior between the audience and the speaker. If somehow you can see me as a person, who in fumbling ways is reaching out to you as an independent spirit, and if I can address myself to real persons and not to a mass of faces, if I can relate to individuals and not to an abstract audience, I will have taken the first essential step in encounter. This cannot be done by talking about individuality, by studying mass society as if it were something out there unrelated to each of us, nor can it be realized by mere understanding of the problems of identity and how to cope with them. Sometimes we begin in this way, but an impersonal or an intellectual approach hinders more often than it helps.

A recent survey of college students indicated that a high percentage of students want to be told what they should do and when they should do it, believing that direction from appropriate authorities is the best way to prepare for future jobs. Further, the study indicated that students lack confidence in their own ideas, thoughts, and values; they are reluctant to express their own opinions and convictions or to participate in class beyond volunteering facts that they are sure of and ideas that instructors want them to express or that instructors agree with. Students want to be told what the right answers are and what to learn because they believe that, by acquiring appropriate information and knowledge, they, too, will become experts and thereby achieve status and economic security. When the student gives the "right" answer, whether he believes it or not, he is rewarded with the valued grade symbol. Thus the student's values are shifted to the outside. As Rollo May has pointed out: "He is validated by scores; he experiences himself of worth only in terms of a series of marks on a technical scale. This shift of validation to the outside shrinks his consciousness and undermines his experience of himself. And again it is not simply that the criteria are external (we all must live, at whatever stage, by many external criteria) but rather the criteria are not *chosen by the person himself* but brought to bear upon him by others, in this case parents and school authorities."

Such an educational process takes the student further and further away from his own self. Being directed by external signs and symbols and being motivated by external rewards are acts of self-denial very similar to the self-denial and estrangement of early life, when the child is taught that his parents are the authorities in the home; they are the statement-makers and the ones who know; thus he sets his sights on achieving their standards and expectations and gives up the judgment of his own senses. He may become shrewd, calculating, and cynical, or he may simply become apathetic and passive.

The conforming person is often the "good" person whose primary mode of existence is rooted in others; the "other" becomes the center of the world. It requires intelligence to know what another expects of you, to be aware of the other's values and preferences; it requires intelligence to develop reactive abilities, to know what other people want and believe and care about. And the most intelligent persons are apt to be the most successful in tuning in on others' requirements and expectations and in achieving the approved goals.

Submission and telling people what they want to hear are rewarded with attention, recognition, approval, privilege, and status, but there is a price to pay in loss of self-esteem, personal integrity, and meaning in living. As long as the right signs are given from the outside, as long as someone is conditioning the person for what is expected and rewarding him for doing the right things, he appears to be comfortable, secure, and content. But as soon as there is no external stimulation and direction, as soon as external rewards cease to have meaning, the person becomes confused, for having given up his own individuality, his own response to life, he experiences little knowledge of who he is, what he wants, and what his real feelings are. Such a person has lost touch with the actual both in himself and in others; he is unable to distinguish between the genuine and the counterfeit.

In an alienating climate, learning becomes largely mechanical and the individual ceases to exist; he fails to realize that genuine learning is often an aching, struggling, solitary process, that innovations and original directions grow from the self, that true learning ultimately involves unique perceptions and unique integrations, and that real expertness is more a light from within, more a matter of personal wisdom and the making of good choices, than the ability to reproduce facts. The creative individual begins with his own senses, feelings, and experiences and centers his world in himself and not in others.

The reactive man who looks for others' opinions and standards as his guide has lost touch with his own sources for creative growth. Knowledge, when it is external to the self and unrelated to it, has value only as a series of abstractions, but it has no transforming meaning for the individual; it has no real impact on the person where he lives most deeply, within himself. In this form, knowledge is an intellectual exercise of temporary value—as all of us know who have crammed for exams dealing with topics that have no real significance and that are quickly forgotten or dispensed with when the course is over.

To remain an individual it is necessary to keep in touch with oneself; that is, to be aware of one's own response to life, not to become detached, cold, withdrawn, objective, in the narrow sense, but to stay open, to feel, to observe, explore, and know—not merely about the various issues, concepts, problems, and themes relevant to man and the universe—but to stay within knowledge and experience as a spontaneous, personal, receptive being. To know the meaning of individuality, one must be an individual while, at the same time, remaining aware of what constitutes one's own individuality—not simply in loneliness and solitude, where the challenge to know and to become is within the person, but also in person-to-person meetings, where there is always a choice between wearing a mask and becoming counterfeit or being authentic and facing the reality of conflict and genuine encounter.

A potential bridge of meaning always exists between the knower and the known, but this reality is elusive and discovering it requires the unique presence of the individual. This presence is not an exclusive matter; it includes pathways of relatedness that bridge the distance between the single, solitary self and the other person. Being truly individual can be a completely private and isolating reality in certain settings and in certain places and times. But as long as others are in one's personal world, a bridge of meaning must be formed which somehow includes the other, which somehow transcends individuality without denying or violating it; somehow the space between the one and the other must be filled with uniqueness, with identity, with individual presence, while, at the same time, making a person-to-person connection and entering into joint life with others. Otherwise, all we have is an eccentric self, alienated and cut off from others—an immature self, pursuing whims and fancies for purely hedonistic and narcissistic ends. Or we have the external, which can be mimicked, copied, and repeated. Between the authentic and the counterfeit, there is always a choice, regardless of past history and experience—the choice of whether to conform and take on the preferences and actions of the other or to allow one's own senses to perceive, to sift, and to conclude. There is always the choice between making knowledge personal and, therefore, meaningful, relevant and alive, and the basis for encounter with others or making it impersonal, like the dead facts on the dead pages of a dead book.

Spontaneity is another component of individuality; it always involves a certain quality of imagination, daring, and risk, a forward-moving quality of the self, in which an individual plunges into new areas, tries out new experiences, and ventures into the unknown. In spontaneous moments the individual simply lets go, freely, with his whole self, as an artist throws himself into a painting or a jazz musician creates his theme, as an infant immerses himself in the world of shape and color and movement. Spontaneity means losing one's self as a separate other yet remaining absolutely related to the moment, whether in poetry or dance or music or an idea, or even in meditation and silence. But while the controlling conscious side is lost, the uniqueness of the individual, the most distinctive characteristics of the self, shines forth. One lets go of external structure, of extraneous rules, of the system, and in doing so the essence of the person comes through. Then the reality being experienced is a personal reality based on one's own senses, like seeing for the first time; then the individual is not determined by others but only by his own experience.

Most of our living in a competitive, technological society is motivated by a need to establish an identification, which includes rank, status, and achievement. Identifications fix the person in society and define him by categories, comparisons, and evaluations, which in a very real sense alienate the person from others and from himself. Identifications are forms of role-playing and ways of wearing different masks that bear little relationship to persons as individuals. We identify the person by comparing him with others, and through comparison and evaluation we judge his worth in rank, status, and position. Every identification carries with it certain labels—professor, honor student, husband, wife, president, secretary, Negro, white, doctor, teacher, Republican, Democrat, excellent, average. Through these labels and through other classifications we come to know about the person; we come to know his place in the hierarchy. In the various institutions of society—the family, the school, the church, business, industry, and government —we ask questions that will help us to label and classify —name, address, telephone number, marital status, education, and much, much more. But data that identify masses of people tell us nothing of the real person behind the data—his interests, his perceptions, his feelings, what significance various social, economic, and psychological factors have in his everyday world; these facts tell us nothing of the real meaning of his existence. To know what it means to be culturally deprived, to be displaced, to be neurotic or psychotic, to be Catholic or Mormon, to be a Negro or a Jew, to be married or single, to be a doctor or a teacher, or any of the other labels we attach to men, we must know the man in direct, open experience; we must know the person as an integrated human being, through his own perceptions, his desires, hopes, and fears, his beliefs, and his values. We must know him in the real places of his living—in the hours when he sits alone, defeated and in despair; in the days when he knows vitality, excitement, and beauty; in his experiences with people when he is free to be himself; in the days of darkness and gloom as well as in the times of joy and happiness. We must know him in a range of significant experiences, in a range of emotions —anger, sadness, excitement, failure, and triumph; in the moments of silence and solitude; in problems, in tragedy, in agony and struggle, in boredom and tranquility, in all the existential moments that distinguish real life from death and the ego chill.

The labels we attach to people, the names and all the other things that identify the individual by distinguishing him from the masses, are just what prevent genuine knowing. For labels and classifications make it appear that we know the other, when actually we have caught the shadow and not the substance. Since we are convinced we know ourselves and others, since we take this knowledge for granted, we fail to recognize that our perceptions are only habits growing out of routines and familiar patterns of expression. We no longer actually see what is happening before us and in us, and, not knowing that we do not know, we make no effort to be in contact with the real. We continue to use labels to stereotype ourselves and others, and these labels have replaced human meanings, unique feelings, and growing life within and between persons.

The more categories into which we can place the individual and the more traits we assign to him, the more we create barriers to authentic knowing and authentic communication. The facts about a person that help to map him on a chart are ways of identifying, but they do not disclose the real identity of the person, for identity is the particular nature of the man, the essential character of his being; it is those components which make him unlike any other person—his special feelings, his ways of perceiving, his peculiar interests, his desires and dreams and the unique flavor of those desires and interests and dreams, his style—in a word, his essence. Identity grows from peculiar capacities and talents, from the sources of life that hold significance and meaning for the individual, from the sources of life that challenge the person to express his real being, from situations and moments that provoke and captivate attention and compel the individual to respond from within—excitement, daring, risk, vivacity, involvement as a total self, in silence, in dialogue, in communication.

Even a person's name, which is the final distinguishing characteristic, is not essential in identity; it is only a fact of identification. And, like other comparative and distinguishing labels that are assigned from the outside, it reveals nothing of the real person. Of course, my name may be spoken as "thou" and not as "it," that is, spoken in the personal, with love that mirrors a total identity. Then it is not just a label but a reflection of deep human meaning, compassionate and tender.

In many ways, however, my name creates barriers to genuine communication. Nothing is more frustrating or alienating for me than to meet people who hear my name and talk to me as if I were not there as an alive, breathing person, but only as if I were that idea or theory, people who treat me as if I were the book or article I wrote, people who talk about me as if I were not present, in the immediate moment, ready and open for a new meeting or adventure, which I cannot experience through past statements but only by coming face to face with this new person and by coming to know him in concrete, personal interaction.

I am not that name on the letter the postman brings. I am not the author of that book. These are facts about me, but they are not me. And when, in the eyes of the postman, I become that letter; when, in the eyes of a reader, I become that man who wrote a book, or the book itself; when, in the mind of a physician, I become that defective or diseased part, I am denied my individuality and I am restrained from real meeting. I am blocked from the actual, which alone can lead to genuine living.

Sometimes I just want to break out into the open, break loose, free, and do something wild and crazy, something in madness that will suddenly shock and dissipate the fixation, the labeling, the detachment and classification, something like entering into an emotional fugue and making weird vibrations, something that will put an end to all the false mannerisms and all the false gestures and faces that people employ in their contacts with each other, something that will dispel the expectations and definitions of others and let the flow of authentic life return.

Although identifications are necessary to carry out some of the activities in a complex society, we have forgotten that, at best, these are instruments or means for facilitating, and we have made them the basis for behavior and interaction. Instead of being reference points, they have become the actualities.

Identity refers to the essential nature of reality; it is

whatever it is that constitutes being; it is the actual, living substance. It is not what distinguishes and compares; it is not my place in the competitive and status hierarchies; for these tell what people are like and unlike, not who they are. Further, these facts objectify and turn people into things, and then the things themselves become the objects of our attention and communication.

The identity of the person is that which exists as real, as vital, as authentically present. It is that which is integral, unique, and gives meaning to activity. It is not a thing to be analyzed and explained, or parts to be defined and labeled, but rather a substance to be sensed and a process to be felt; it is a special reality in the unchanging, persistent nature of integral form, yet it is a reality that involves ever-changing expressions.

Individuality and identity emerge from the deep levels of the self, from the resources and talents that exist in each of us to be formed and shaped into a particular being in the world. It is these values which society should recognize, encourage, and affirm. The self cannot develop unless there is freedom, choice, and responsibility, unless each person experiences his own senses and becomes an active force in life, free to choose and select, free to feel and express openly and honestly the nature of these feelings, free to identify with living forces, with alive persons who encourage growth in individual identity, who value being for itself, and who can enable the person to engage himself and be committed to meaningful inquiry and activity.

Individuality in its purest form is a mark of distinctiveness unlike any other living form; it is life emerging from peculiar perceptions; it is an expression of the self that leads to an awakening from within and a knowing of what one wants in life and what registers as worthwhile or meaningless. In its fullest sense and varied forms, individuality is the good that each man seeks in days of darkness and in days of light. To be the way I am constructed to be, to be who I am, is both the expression of absolute value and value itself.

In times when individual values are being grossly denied, when I become discouraged with rejection, violence, and avarice, when I become depressed with the forces of man that destroy the self and separate and divide, that move man one more step toward alienation and dehumanization, I return to my own self, to silence and solitude.

There is perhaps only one way to come to terms with these feelings of despair—somehow to express something of the almost overwhelming agony I experience. The words that immediately come are "a deadness of spirit," a kind of inner dying and the pain of seeing around me ongoing life, being in touch with it, sensitive and caring, yet deep down a decaying spirit, growing out of the pulls in many directions and the feeling of being fragmented and torn by the impossibility of continually maintaining my own individuality, by the impossibility of living in different worlds at the same time and fervently wanting to be in touch with everyone—yes, to be, to see, to feel, to love everyone. It is the impossibility of being with the one and with the other, without somehow losing myself, of being pulled and divided by loyalties, split by forces outside yet staying with myself and remaining true to my own being. In such moments I feel the absolute impossibility of identity. Somewhere back in the mountains in a ravine I tossed myself in aching horror, and unknown, strange sounds came hissing from my body and reverberated against the walls of the mountain. I knew within me the extreme feeling of dying; the sounds that came were cries of loneliness and helplessness in a world of irresolvable human struggle. It was as though one half of me could find the beauty in the woods, the movement of the trees, the wind, the patterns of light and darkness, love and the other half could know only the shrill sounds, the breaking branches, the hatred and hostility and the tearing away of life. At such times it is torture to find the higher truth, when being true will tend to cancel out the one person or the other. Perhaps there is no answer to this dilemma but to recognize the inevitability of human conflict and crisis and to know that while part of the spirit of relationship is dying a new dimension of my own individual self is being born. I know now that to love, to relate, to encounter, no matter how totally, leads ultimately to pain, that establishing a community among strangers or among friends is a lifelong challenge bound to create division, strife, struggle, and suffering. When each person feels he knows the truth and fails to listen to the voice of others, something human closes between persons like a shadow coming between them, like a wall, sometimes like a poison, which permeates the atmosphere and constricts human hearts and loves. It is a terribly painful experience to see individuals one loves lose their human feeling for one another, their roots in a relationship, and to hear each strongly proclaim the validity of his perception of reality, without really listening to the other, without really caring. To be in the midst of just this battle among individuals, struggling to be and really to value the presence of each one, to see divisiveness and alienation and not be able to leap beyond it and find a bridge of meaning and relatedness (without denying the one or the other), this for me is the great human tragedy. In the depths of this despair, I do not want to hear another human voice or see another human face; I want to be away from human life, isolated and lonely; but after a while I return, because without other human beings, there is no reason for living, without the existence of others, life is absurd and meaningless and I can never be completely whole. I search once more for vitality, beauty, excitement, and human value, first in music, in art, in poetry, in dance, and in nature, and then once more with other people. Sometimes an exquisite poem, such as this by William Alexander Percy, arouses a new spirit and thirst for life in me.

### Home[1]

I have a need of silence and of stars;
Too much is said too loudly; I am dazed.
The silken sound of whirled infinity
Is lost in voices shouting to be heard.
I once knew men as earnest and less shrill.
An undermeaning that I caught I miss
Among these ears that hear all sounds save silence,
These eyes that see so much but not the sky,
These minds that gain all knowledge but no calm.
If suddenly the desperate music ceased,
Could they return to life? or would they stand
In dancers' attitudes, puzzled, polite,
And striking vaguely hand on tired hand
For an encore, to fill the ghastly pause?
I do not know. Some rhythm there may be
I cannot hear. But I—oh, I must go
Back where the breakers of deep sunlight roll
Across flat fields that love and touch the sky;
Back to the more of earth, the less of man,
Where there is still a plain simplicity,
And friendship, poor in everything but love,
And faith, unwise, unquestioned, but a star.
Soon now the peace of summer will be there
With cloudy fire of myrtle in full bloom;
And, when the marvelous wide evenings come,
Across the molten river one can see
The misty willow-green of Arcady.
And then—the summer stars . . . I will go home.

### REFERENCES

Danskin, David G., Foster, James M., and Kennedy, Carroll E., Jr. *Attitudes and Ambitions of College Students.* Manhattan, Kansas: Kansas State University, Bulletin 479, January, 1965.

Huxley, Aldous. "Education on the Non-Verbal Level," *Daedalus,* 91:279, Spring 1962.

Kesey, Ken. *One Flew Over the Cuckoo's Nest.* New York: Viking Press, 1962.

---

[1] Reprinted from *Of Silence and of Stars* by William Alexander Percy. Copyright 1953, by permission of LeRoy P. Percy, Greenville, Mississippi.

May, Rollo. *Psychology and the Human Dilemma.* Princeton, New Jersey: D. Van Nostrand Co., 1966.

Moustakas, Clark. *The Authentic Teacher.* Cambridge, Massachusetts: Howard A. Doyle Publishing Co., 1966.

Moustakas, Clark. *Creativity and Conformity.* Princeton, New Jersey: D. Van Nostrand Co., 1967.

Percy, William Alexander. "Home," *Of Silence and of Stars.* Greenville, Mississippi: Levye Press, 1953.

CHAPTER 2

# *Loneliness*

# *and*

# *Solitude*

To remain in touch with oneself as an individual requires an awareness of the conditions in society that threaten to chain man to a life of security and comfort, to a life of habit and routine, where feelings are modulated and disguised. Once a fixed pattern of living is established, the person only dimly perceives his own inner response to experience, his own real thoughts and feelings. He only vaguely notices that increasing regularity exacts a penalty of monotony and dullness and that organization and efficiency often lead to boredom. When one really looks, one sees the same faces and voices, the same pathways, the same motions and actions, appearing and reappearing. The routine nature of existence may not be recognized, but the alarm clock puts modern man into motion in the morning and into bed at night, and the same old roads are being traveled.

As long as habit and routine dictate the pattern of living, new dimensions of the self will not emerge; new interests will not develop. The human scene becomes one of still life, where familiar images become commonplace and words and gestures repeat a well-known refrain. In such a state, it takes a sudden jolt to shock the person into an awareness that his existence is basically mechanical and dead. It often takes a severe threat to make one aware of one's failure to be, of one's failure to discover new meaning and value in living. The sudden recognition that daily life has become petrified in order to achieve security and to establish a steady, stable existence may produce severe anxiety. When the person is alone and considers the real nature of his existence, when he becomes aware of the emptiness of his life, he stands mute before himself. He discovers what really matters in shaping new meanings and directions to his life. In solitude, the person often reaches almost wordless states of experience and a vividness of inner life in aesthetic and spiritual forms. Here is an example of an experience of solitude in nature that a student recently shared with me:

> While watching a sunset during a vesper service, I discovered the peace and tranquility of nature. The sun slipped behind the distant mountain tops as I watched, enraptured. The mystical murmurings of the trees added a ghostly quality to the gentle sound of singing which flowed lazily toward me on the wings of the wind. In the valley everything seemed serene and carefree. A chipmunk scurried across a rock and birds called soothing messages to their mates. I could not bear to shatter the sacred silence of the sky or to veil the sounds of nature behind those of man. I sat silently watching the ancient ritual of the wild as the world prepared for nightfall with its slumber and rest.

Solitude is a return to one's own self when the world has grown cold and meaningless, when life has become filled with people and too much of a response to others. Solitude is as much an intrinsic desire in man as his gregariousness. Hermits, solitary thinkers, independent spirits, recluses, although often stigmatized in the modern world, are healthy expressions of man's dialogue with himself. The overdevelopment of socialized man, the constant need for involvement with people, is often motivated by a fear of discovering one's own real self and by the anxiety of remaining stagnant in the presence of surrounding life. Socialized man too often lacks the courage to become more profoundly aware, to stretch his resources to new levels, and to participate in the mystery of living, which is ineffable, indescribable, unpredictable, and, in some ways, private and unsharable. The response to others, however meaningful or meaningless, can be broken only through solitude. It is unlike any other experience—not to have to respond to others, not to be stimulated or challenged by others, just to be alone.

In solitude man does not deal with concrete and practical realities, for being practical is simply another way of socializing, of submitting or disclosing one's secrets in material ways, of giving statements that can be counted, explained, and analyzed. The truly solitary process is not tangible and materialistic; it cannot be defined and quantified. It remains aesthetic and mystical and forms in feeling and spirit. The moment it is studied and "understood" it becomes something else, something radically unlike the original solitude, with all its vague, diffuse visions and dreams, with all its imagining and wondering and its incomprehensible powers that sensitize and cleanse. In the process the individual often purges himself of false idols, distortions, and deceptions; he creates a new picture of reality and reaches for the truth. The moment of solitude is a spontaneous, awakening experience, a coming to life in one's own way, a path to authenticity and self-renewal.

## LARA AND DEATH

An example of solitude in facing the problem of separation and death is Lara's visit to the funeral home for the final encounter with Doctor Zhivago. Here we see the significance of self-reflection, meditation, and dialogue, the continuity of life in the face of death, of ongoing meaning in the presence of an apparent end of a relationship, of self-confrontation and struggle and determination to keep on living and growing, to keep on loving and valuing in a relationship—more than this, to find new awareness and meaning.

In this autobiographical moment, Lara has just entered the room where Doctor Zhivago's body is displayed for mourning friends and relatives. People pour into the room to offer respect and tribute to the dead man. But Lara is really not aware of anyone else; she does not hear the voices or the painful sobs, nor does she see the grief-stricken, mourning faces; she does not hear the shuffling of the crowd, the coughs of the men, or the cries of the women. She is alone with herself—the beating of her heart, the images and reveries of rich moments once shared and reflections on the future that involve, too, the carrying forward of her love for Yurii and the values and dreams she shares with him. She reaches, temporarily, the very bottom of her misery, but at the same time there is a feeling in this room with Yurii of life being lived, of love being experienced in all its joy and sadness. She is enveloped momentarily in the air of a freedom and unconcern that emanates from him, and something incomprehensible is happening to her; she is breaking free into the open, with Yurii's help, out of sorrows that imprison her and into the joy of liberation. Sequences of ideas, insights, truths, feelings drift and sail freely through her, like clouds in the sky— rich dialogue and a spontaneous understanding that is warm, instinctive, immediate. In Pasternak's words:

> Oh, what a love it was, utterly free, unique, like nothing else on earth! Their thoughts were like other people's songs.
> They loved each other, not driven by necessity, by the "blaze of passion" often falsely ascribed to love. They loved each other because everything around them willed it, the trees and the clouds and the sky over their heads and the earth under their feet. Perhaps their surrounding world, the strangers they met in the street, the wide expanses they saw on their walks, the rooms in which

they lived or met, took more delight in their love than they themselves did.

Ah, that was just what had united them and had made them so akin! Never, never, even in their moments of richest and wildest happiness, were they unaware of a sublime joy in the total design of the universe, a feeling that they themselves were a part of that whole, an element in the beauty of the cosmos.

This unity with the whole was the breath of life to them. And the elevation of man above the rest of nature, the modern coddling and worshipping of man, never appealed to them. A social system based on such a false premise, as well as its political application, struck them as pathetically amateurish and made no sense to them.

And now she took her leave of him, addressing him in the direct language of everyday life. Her speech, though lively and informal, was not down-to-earth. Like the choruses and monologues of ancient tragedies, like the language of poetry or music, or any other conventional mode of expression, its logic was not rational but emotional. The rhetorical strain in her effortless, spontaneous talk came from her grief. Her simple, unsolemn words were drenched in tears. It was these tears that seemed to hold her words together in a tender, quick whispering like the rustling of silky leaves in a warm, windy rain.

The worst thing that can happen to these sources of spiritual life and feeling, these private moments, is that they be formulated into principles, creeds, theories, and techniques to be tapped for laboratory or clinical use. When solitude becomes legitimatized or scheduled into life, with appropriate places and methods, its meaning and essence will be destroyed. For solitude is an art form not just for seers and portents and not for professional seekers of truth. It comes and goes in its own valid moments as a capacity of man that is self-initiated but at the same time spontaneous and free. One does not classify and explain the ineffable, the peaks and valleys of heaven and hell; one does not concretize the vastness of space and time, the infinity of earth and sky.

Solitude is man's organic tie to himself and to the universe.

In real solitude we are expansive, limitless, free. We do not disguise our feelings from ourselves, but rather we renew contact with ourselves and discover who we are. At other times we are pulled into the collective stream that surrounds us. We experience the collective sense that we have incorporated in order to achieve recognition, security, and comfort. In solitude, one breaks through the dead, static patterns and has an opportunity to see life as it really is and to become aware of a desire for new meaning, excitement, and vitality, of a desire to be whole and to live more fully and completely.

Important as it is, at times, solitude is not enough to break new ground, to challenge the mechanical nature of existence, to confront life with a new reality, or to come to grips with the pain of isolation, rejection, and death. Solitude contributes to awareness and change; it creates the setting or climate, but often it does not carry out the theme. Dissatisfaction with life and awareness of new possibilities are sometimes not enough to create a new world. Often it is necessary that the person feel the anguish of loneliness, that he feel cut off from the sources of genuine life, that he feel the agony of loss of human meaning, and that he know the tragic separation from his own self. It is important that the person feel the emptiness of existence all the way, in the depths of his being, and know that his deadness of spirit may be more related to his failure to live honestly than to outside pressure and defeat. It is important, too, that the individual recognize the basic loneliness of individuality, the basic loneliness of separateness, and let these feelings stand.

Loneliness and solitude are sometimes used as synonyms. According to Webster's Third New International Dictionary, loneliness means without company, solitary, not frequented by human beings, alone. From the same source, solitude is defined as a state of being alone, remote from society, lonely. While I do not believe that meaning is derived by defining terms in this way, it is important to recognize that loneliness and solitude are different though closely related experiences.

I prefer to consider loneliness and solitude in terms of the kinds of experiences that arouse these feelings. Loneliness is often connected with feelings of rejection, with feelings of guilt for not being who one is and for not actualizing one's potentialities; it occurs in the presence of tragedy, disease, illness, and death; it is associated with a new truth that suddenly shatters old perceptions or ideas; it is connected with feeling different from other members of a group or feeling misunderstood and apart from others, with a sense of not belonging. It is frequently associated with broken relationships and separation experiences. There are many, many kinds of loneliness, but each experience is unique and each represents a different moment of life.

Here are some examples. First, Margarethe Wiest's poem of the loneliness of feeling accepted and loved for the first time:

> Like birds in winter
> You fed me;
> Knowing the ground was frozen,
> Knowing
> I should never come to your hand,
> Knowing
> You did not need my gratitude.
>
> Softly,
> Like snow falling on snow,
> Softly, so not to frighten me,
> Softly
> You threw your crumbs on the ground
> and walked away,
> Waiting.

The loneliness of death is expressed in this letter from a friend:

All the vivid details of my experience of loneliness are still with me as if it had happened only yesterday. There was a long-distance call for me. My heart sank.

This was a loneliness I had never known before—the telephone booth closed in on me and it was almost as if I weren't breathing at all. *It was all so final!* I would never see my friend again. Religion at that moment was not enough to help me. I simply wept and wept and let go completely.

I don't remember how I spent Saturday. On Easter Sunday I attended church in a strange city, but the minister seemed to have something to say to me. I felt better, but still lonely. All this time I was fortunate enough to be traveling with another very good friend. Though I was not alone, I was lonely. It was a most unusual day, and unforgettable.

There were redbud and flowering shrubs, bright new green grass, red-bricked and white-pillared colonial buildings of Hanover College in stark relief against the threatening dark sky; the sunshine made all things brighter and sharply outlined in contrast. Billowing white clouds were moving fast, piling up high against slate ones with the rays of the sun breaking through intermittently. It was one of those hot, humid days when delicate odors were more noticeable, bird notes more clear—the freshness and newness of life was all around me—it was breathtakingly beautiful. I felt momentarily one with God and my friend; I was no longer lonely. The Easter message was for me, too, and I felt I really understood somehow the truer meaning of life in death.

Then, as if all this beauty were not enough, I found a double rainbow for an anticlimax. The heavens had opened and the rain had drenched the earth. When the sun came again I followed the bands of brilliant color clear across the sky into the ground below me where the wide expanses of the Ohio River rolled brown with the muds of Spring. The unreal, brightly reflected light made that part of the valley where fields were already tilled and planted a lasting painting for my mind's eye. One of the loneliest moments of my life I found the most beautiful, meaningful, and haunting I have ever experienced. I remember this feeling in an inexplainable way —sadness and longing mingled with an appreciation and awareness of beauty and a depth of emotion which was rare and inspiring.

There are times now when a lovely sunset, the scent of clover or sweet grass in June, a scarlet tanager in the tip of a tamarack, hoar frost in full moonlight in January in the quiet north woods, great symphonic music, a hermit thrush in the silence and fragrance of dusk in the jack pine plains, an unguarded expression on a loved one's face, a loon frantically calling in the mist of the early morning—these things once shared with those I love— fleetingly give me that feeling of what I call loneliness. I believe that whenever any experience is too beautiful to phrase into words, I feel loneliness.

## THE LONELINESS OF REJECTED LOVE

The loneliness of rejection is portrayed in the following theme written by a tenth-grade boy.

Loneliness is a depressing state of mind that none de- sires but we all endure. When I'm lonely it's not because of being shut away from human beings physically but when I'm rejected from those I respect and love. If a close friend turns against me I feel hurt and lonely. When I feel like a square block in a round hole, it brings on a form of loneliness. Sometimes my parents seem unfair; there is no one to turn to and I feel desolate, lost. Loneliness comes every day. When someone makes a thoughtless criticism that attacks one of my weaknesses, it takes the wind out of my sails. I wonder if what they say is really true. I get a small feeling and that's a kind of loneliness.

Then there is another kind of loneliness—the kind to be desired. When I experience something new and won- derful, a new thrill, I like to be alone where I can think it over, remember every part of it. I like to bathe in those happy memories. That's a satisfying loneliness. Whether I'm in a happy, gratified or desolate, depressed state of mind, loneliness is an important facet of my life.

## LONELINESS OF SEPARATION

The loneliness of separation is perceived as a negative experience in the following essay of a tenth-grade girl:

Loneliness gives me a cold feeling like the loneliness the earth feels in winter when the birds and flowers have left her, and I feel as though I don't have a friend in the world. The whole house is lifeless now and that makes me feel depressed. Depression is truly a part of this feeling of loneliness. It has no joy or excitement in it as houses blessed with a happy and loving family usually do. There never seems to be anything to do. It all seems to be done, it is as if you were trapped in a strange world of loneliness, a world in which you are caught up in a great vacuum of emptiness.

A related kind of separation experience is expressed by Donna Turley in this longing for a return of intimate social relations and friendships once known, in this desire for love that cannot be.

That deep and abiding longing I so often of late find harboring within myself . . . is now moving near the heart of me again . . . and while I listen hard enough to hear the most distant sound I can strain myself to find, it is a mellow and a mournful and a sad melody . . . a profound hurting . . . a painful coming to newness.

Faint sounds of those I love are intermingled with tones that remind me of the somberest moments of my life. Oh! there's so much, so very much lost love . . . so far and wide has my caring been thrown . . . so seldom to take root and truly grow. And there's even a mournfulness in the places where it has grown most strongly and flowered most beautifully . . . because it is such a miracle that I want to come much, much nearer to it than there is space to squeeze into.

I somehow want to still be holding those seeds in the palm of my hand . . . though they could never have taken root and grown into relationship and meaning had I not let them go . . . but now I cannot ever retrieve them. Oh! this longing, the distant bells and the deep and penetrating surges as I contemplate all . . . all I've given . . . all I found and reached eagerly toward another with . . . and all that happened then . . . the ignoring, the misinterpretation, the forgetting, the blindness . . . so much has fallen out of my grasp into the void as I attempted to give it.

Sadness also reeks all around that which was felt, seen, held, treasured, and loved . . . because for this to have happened, I had to let it go from me . . . and it had to change and grow and expand . . . and the paltry little I once fondly held and timidly extended . . . that little treasure can never exist the same again.

The loss, the missing, the emptiness . . . it is all inevitable to one who lives and gives. The longing for all those I love, the half-dying for want of that old touch or glance . . . that same familiar knowingness and those hands and eyes . . . which so many past times saw and felt and knew me. Those brows so often once knitted with my pain and sorrow and those worn hands which once held so much that was dear to me . . . which once were within my own reach . . . and I could take them and hold them as tightly and as long as I wished . . . now where are they? Where could I go to gather together all my loves and all my caring ones and all the pieces of my gifts, and all my sources of strength?

This exquisite sadness of knowing they can never be brought again in one and known on the simple daily basis once possible . . . this pierces the being of me. Tear away half of my being and I couldn't feel more separated and incomplete.

I am haunted by all the pairs of eyes which once held tears and looks and recognitions and caresses for me . . . but they are spread and diverged through the immensity of space now.

Paul Tillich believed that two words were created in the English language to express the two sides of man's aloneness—"loneliness" to express pain in being alone and "solitude" to express the glory of being alone. As Tillich saw it, loneliness is most widespread when we are left alone through separation or death, but it also occurs in those moments when the person feels absolutely isolated or misunderstood or when he remains silent and withdrawn though surrounded by people he loves. There is also the loneliness of disappointed love or rejected love; and, finally, there is the loneliness of guilt (the failure to be) and the loneliness of having to die, of anticipating death in the actual day or hour of our dying.

Solitude takes other forms: the desire toward the silence of nature—we speak without voice to the trees and the clouds and the waves of the sea—or the solitude of listening to poetry, or reading it, or listening to music, or viewing works of art. At such times we are alone even in the midst of crowds, but we are not lonely. Silence is an essential part of solitude; in silence there is a self-conscious, careful perceiving within, unlike any other reality, deep and pervasive, leaving its own distinctive mark. The real silence, says Maeterlinck, surrounds us on every side and is the source of the undercurrents of life. What is the innermost nature of solitude? Tillich answers as follows: "The presence of the eternal upon the crowded roads of the temporal. It is the experience of being alone but not lonely . . . to face the eternal, to find others, to see ourselves." Although Tillich believed one can overcome loneliness through solitude, he saw this only as a temporary condition; inevitably, loneliness returns in the face of boredom, emptiness, deviance, rejection, separation, illness, and death, even in the face of love. For love itself can be lonely—more than that, it may even intensify the sense of loneliness, as it did for Rufus and his father in *Death in the Family*. Here loneliness and solitude mingle together to deepen and extend individuality and the sense of community. Rufus and his father share an evening walk, quietly, slowly, anticipating the event, savoring it and finding a strange tranquility in it. They sit on a rock, each experiencing a kind of contentment unlike any other he has known. Rufus, in this quiet place, suddenly understands his father; he realizes that, although his father loves their home and all of them, he is more lonely than this family love can help; the love of his family increases his loneliness and makes it hard for him not to be lonely; but on the rock he feels completely himself and is on good terms with his loneliness. An important part of this feeling of love and communion between Rufus and his father comes from their being together away from home, sharing together moments of solitude and meditation, very quietly, in the dark, listening to the leaves and looking at the stars. Agee puts it this way:

> These realizations moved clearly through the senses, the memory, the feelings, the mere feeling of the place they paused at, about a quarter of a mile from home, on a rock under a stray tree that had grown in the city, their feet on undomesticated clay . . . above them, the trembling lanterns of the universe seeming so near, so intimate, that when air stirred the leaves and their hair, it seemed to be breathing, the whispering of the stars. Sometimes on these evenings his father would hum a little and the humming would break open into a word or two, but he never finished even a part of a tune, for silence was even more pleasurable. . . . Rufus felt his father's hand settle, without groping, or clumsiness, on the top of his bare head; it took his forehead and smoothed it, and pushed the hair backward from his forehead, and held the back of his head while Rufus pressed his head backward against the firm hand, and, in reply to that pressure, clasped over his right ear and cheek, over the whole side of the head, and drew Rufus' head quietly and strongly against the sharp cloth that covered his father's body, through which Rufus could feel the breathing ribs; then relinquished him. . . . he saw that his father's eyes had become still more clear and grave and that the deep lines around his mouth were satisfied; and looked up at what his father was so steadily looking at, at the leaves which silently breathed and at the stars which beat like hearts. He heard a long sigh break from his father, and then his father's abrupt voice: "Well . . ." and the hand lifted from him and they both stood up. The rest of the way home they did not speak, or put on their hats.[1]

In contrast to the powerful experience of being lonely, even in the presence of gentler forces, solitude contains basically tranquil tones and themes and ineluctable feelings of dreams and memories, of desires and imaginings.

---

[1] Reprinted from *A Death in the Family* by James Agee. Copyright 1957 by The James Agee Trust, by permission of the publisher, Grosset & Dunlap, Inc., New York.

In solitude there is peace and joy and a sense of the
eternal rhythms of life, a natural beauty that grows and
expands, quietly, like the peaceful movements of a
stream, then suddenly the person is in touch with life
and the mystery in the universe. This is the experience
of the central character in *Green Mansions*. Temporarily
isolated in a forest in the Quenevata Mountains, he
comes upon a single white flower that he has never seen
before, and the exquisite moment in nature comes to
life.

> After I had looked long at it, and passed on, the image
> of that perfect flower remained so persistently in my
> mind that on the following day I went again, in the hope
> of seeing it still untouched by decay. There was no
> change; and on this occasion I spent a much longer time
> looking at it, admiring the marvelous beauty of its form,
> which seemed so greatly to exceed that of all other
> flowers . . . cut by a divinely inspired artist from some
> unknown precious stone, of the size of a large orange
> and whiter than milk, and yet, in spite of its opacity,
> with a crystalline luster on the surface. Next day I went
> again, scarcely hoping to find it still unwithered; it was
> fresh as if only just opened; and after that I went often,
> sometimes at intervals of several days, and still no faint-
> est sign of any change, the clear, exquisite lines still
> undimmed, the purity and luster as I had first seen it.
> . . . it would continue to bloom when I had looked my
> last on it; wind and rain and sunlight would never stain,
> never tinge, its sacred purity; the savage Indian, though
> he sees little to admire in a flower, yet seeing this one
> would veil his face and turn back; even the browsing
> beast crashing his way through the forest, struck with its
> strange glory, would swerve aside and pass on without
> harming it.

Here we see two functions of solitude: the awakening
of the incomprehensible, the essential mystery of human
existence, and the birth of the inexplicable within ourselves. From these dimensions of self coming to life, we
experience a sense of wonder, an awareness that casts
freshness and light, an expansiveness of self, perceiving

vividly and clearly. Hermann Hesse, a truly lonely figure in modern literature, believed that self-awareness could be achieved only through solitude and self-reflection. In *Demian,* he wrote:

> Few people nowadays know what man is. Many sense this ignorance and die the more easily because of it. . . . I do not consider myself less ignorant than most people. I have been and still am a seeker, but I have ceased to question stars and books; I have begun to listen to the teachings my blood whispers to me. My story is not a pleasant one; it is neither sweet nor harmonious as invented stories are; it has the taste of nonsense and chaos, of madness and dreams—like the lives of all men who stop deceiving themselves.
>
> Each man's life represents a road toward himself, an attempt at such a road, the intimation of a path. No man has ever been entirely and completely himself. Yet each one strives to become that—one in an awkward, the other in a more intelligent way, each as best he can. Each man carries the vestiges of his days. Some never become human, remaining frog, lizard, ant. Some are human above the waist, fish below. Each represents a gamble on the part of nature in creation of the human. We all share the same origin, our mothers; all of us come in at the same door. But each of us—experiments of the depths—strives toward his own destiny. We can understand one another; but each of us is able to interpret himself to himself alone.

Solitude and loneliness are not easy paths to take, because inevitably they challenge the stable pattern of existence, and, in the process, questions and doubts are raised about the meaning and the reality of life. In these moments the individual questions the genuineness, the validity of his own existence. Disenchantment with routine, sudden awareness of the emptiness of life rise up in moods of restlessness and boredom. Sometimes man escapes monotony and routine through drugs or alcoholism, but when he takes the direct path to himself and stays on this path he inevitably experiences loneliness and solitude. Hesse puts the matter even more emphatically:

Each man has only one genuine vocation—to find the way to himself. He might end up as poet or madman, as prophet or criminal—that was not his affair, ultimately it was of no concern. His task was to discover his own destiny—not an arbitrary one—and live it out wholly and resolutely within himself. Everything else was only a would-be existence, an attempt at evasion, a flight back to the ideals of the masses, conformity and fear of one's own inwardness. The new vision rose up before me, glimpsed a hundred times, possibly even expressed before but now experienced for the first time by me. I was an experiment on the part of Nature, a gamble within the unknown, perhaps for a new purpose, perhaps for nothing, and my only task was to allow this game on the part of primeval depths to take its course, to feel its will within me and make it wholly mine. That or nothing!

Man strives for new direction; he seeks to find vitality and excitement, and as he does he awakens to new images; the old patterns and bonds are broken. Then the individual is cut off from what he knows, from the ordinary ways of life, and, standing off by himself, looking within, he questions the reality of what he has been perceiving and valuing. When the lonely spirit awakens, the individual questions all the dimensions of his life. Sometimes he discovers that relationships are not what they seem, that what was regarded as essential is more a matter of role and function and definition, that somewhere along the way his life became fixed into a pointless, steady course, that what was exciting and unique has become nothing more than associations repeating themselves, customs re-emerging. When love is a matter of conditioning, it sets like cement; it does not move forward but takes on a fixed shape and becomes chained to habit. Experiencing the full potential of a relationship means exertion, struggle, and a range of feeling and emotion that leads to innovation and renewal.

I have had many experiences in which I entered into my private thoughts in search of new truth and meaning. In such moments, human distance is real, and a lonely figure waits and searches for a light that is not an illusion and a path that will not turn out to be just one more fantasy. I want to know that the step I take is real, that my heartbeat is its own, that my words belong to me, that my ideals have a place in reality. I want to feel my anguish and pain and know that love will not be shattered, that my dreams will survive the moments of doubt and terror. But, at times, life is empty and meaningless and ugly and terribly, terribly denying and isolating. I walk for hours, talking to myself, trying to make sense out of the senselessness and shock. Then I find an isolated spot, I sit under a tree, and waves of feeling assault me, cover me intensely, until I am shattered and my mind is empty of all thought. I wait, mindlessly, for some new hope to emerge, for some sign in the universe to make a new beginning. In a trance, I remain simply present, rooted in nature, and, by some very gradual, mysterious process, I return to a consciousness of my own existence. "Does the way I live really matter?"

To ask the question, to inquire into life, to doubt the sensibility of existence, these are not questions of a disturbed and thwarted mind. These are questions that man will always ask, in sickness and in health, because they are rooted in the organic pattern of life itself. And, because man strives for the infinite, man will forever be frustrated and discouraged, forever doomed to suffer. But in the suffering, in the struggle, in his loneliness and solitude, he achieves his individuality and his identity. When there is a striking failure in life, man will always return to himself, for, ultimately, man is alone. There is no other road but to one's own self, no other meaning but an inner reality awakened in the quiet, desperate hours when one faces the truth, when one is suddenly unbalanced and dizzy from alienation, shame, and hypocrisy. There is no other source of strength but that which exists within the regions of the self and in the mysterious powers of the universe, when one has known the sharp pain of words and feelings used as weapons or the failure of love to create a bridge of meaning between persons. There is no other life but that of the solitary, single self caught up in the shifting currents of society and the needs and demands of other human beings. While it is being lived, the suffering and anguish is unbearable, but, in time, the hurt moves forward into the bliss of liberation and into a new zest for living. And then there is a passionate claim to human existence that brings with it a feeling of community and a knowing that in the lonely hours the return to one's self is a way back to others. The self that does not reach out to encounter and include others is, indeed, still mourning, split, and suffering. One must know the agony of unanswered doubts and questions, the clear visions of loneliness and solitude, and the joy of being born again. Then, coming back to the human community, one must also know the depths of unconditional love, of an existential meaning that creates a bond with others and cancels out the misunderstanding, incomprehension, and barriers to unity and integration.

## REFERENCES

Agee, James. *A Death in the Family*. New York: Avon Books, 1959.

Hesse, Hermann. *Demian*. New York: Harper & Row, 1965.

Hudson, W. H. *Green Mansions*. New York: Alfred A. Knopf, 1959.

Maeterlinck, Maurice. *The Inner Beauty*. London, England: A. L. Humphreys, 1910.

Moustakas, Clark. *Creativity and Conformity*. Princeton, New Jersey: D. Van Nostrand Co., 1967.

Moustakas, Clark. *Loneliness*. Englewood Cliffs, New Jersey: Prentice-Hall, 1961.

Pasternak, Boris. *Dr. Zhivago*. New York: Pantheon, 1958.

Tillich, Paul. *The Eternal Now*. New York: Charles Scribner's Sons, 1963.

Turley, Donna. *Mosaic of My Self*. Cambridge, Massachusetts: Howard A. Doyle Publishing Co. (In Press)

CHAPTER 3

# Loneliness

# and

# Encounter

I wish to discuss three ways in which man expresses significant dimensions of himself, three essential pathways to self-growth and growth in human relations. The first is man's dialogue with himself, his inner response to life and the feeling that comes from self-confirmation. The tapping of one's own senses to determine the nature of experience, to make choices, and to be responsible for oneself is often initiated through solitude and loneliness. The search within for new perspective may be a painful, terrible struggle or it may be tranquil and silent, but when it involves a genuine relationship to one's self, a direction is realized that represents authentic choice. This means shutting off other noises and sounds, and it often means withdrawal, isolation, and total self-absorption.

Awareness and understanding that emerge from my own discovery are very different from insights that come from another, no matter how emphatic or loving the other person is, and no matter how valid the insights are from the standpoint of society. Unless I perceive

---

[1] Sections of this chapter are reprinted from "Loneliness or Encounter" by Clark Moustakas in *Human Potentialities: The Challenge and The Promise*, Herbert Otto Ed.). St. Louis: Warren H. Green, Inc., 1968, by permission of the publisher.

reality from my own senses, I am not being authentic. The love and understanding of others may actually impede growth, because, in some ways (with all the euphoric, expansive possibilities), love and understanding are binding. Every relationship has boundaries and unique functions, while some aspects of self-growth require freedom from duties and ties, require that the person remain with his own inner experience, with his own private perceptions. To know the beauty of a tree, the essential nature of a mountain, the value of color, form, movement, to perceive essence in art, music, poetry, man must perforce go alone in his own solitude and loneliness and open himself to these aesthetic forms. Discovery, preference, interest, and value coming through the confirmation of one's own senses are radically different realities from commitment and awareness that is shaped by the facilitation or intervention of others. There is no substitute for personal knowledge or for sensitivity and feeling that come from self-communion. An excerpt from *Thus Spake Zarathustra* forcefully expresses the necessity of individual truth:

I honor the recalcitrant choosy tongues and stomachs, which have learned to say "I" and "yes" and "no." But to chew and digest everything—that is truly the swine's manner. Always to bray Yea-Yuh—that only the ass has learned, and whoever is of his spirit. . . .

By many ways, in many ways, I reached my truth: it was not on one ladder that I climbed to the height where my eye roams over my distance. And it was only reluctantly that I ever inquired about the way: that always offended my taste. I preferred to question and try out the ways themselves.

A trying and questioning was my every move; and verily, one must also learn to answer such questioning. That, however, is my taste—not good, not bad, but my taste of which I am no longer ashamed and which I have no wish to hide.

"This is *my* way; where is yours?"—thus I answered those who asked me "the way." For *the* way—that does not exist.

One cannot ultimately know himself through the diagnoses and definitions of others, and one cannot know another person ultimately except by being there in the life of the other, listening, perceiving, waiting for significant aspects of the other person to be expressed and unfold. Steeping oneself in the world of the other and letting one's perceptions take root directly from the expressions of the other are ways of knowing the other as the person he is.

In the interhuman realm, the word "truth" means that men communicate directly who they are. This does not require that the one convey to the other everything that occurs to him, but only that no seeming, no facade, creep in between the one person and the other. It does not depend on one letting oneself go before another, but on the one person granting the other a share in his being. Where authenticity of the interhuman is not found, the human element itself has been violated. Something essential is lacking—a sense of mutuality, a real communication of person to person. This can be achieved in no other way but through the genuine presence of one individual to the other. In *The Mystery of Being*, Marcel comments: "When somebody's presence does really make itself felt, it can refresh my inner being; it reveals me to myself, it makes me more fully myself than I should be if I were not exposed to its impact." In *Between Man and Man*, Buber emphasizes the person-to-person value even more strongly:

> The fundamental fact of human existence is neither the individual as such nor the aggregate as such. Each, considered in itself, is a mighty abstraction. The individual is a fact of existence in so far as he steps into a living relation with other individuals. The aggregate is a fact of existence in so far as it is built up of living units of relation. The fundamental fact of human existence is man with man. What is peculiarly characteristic of the human world is above all that something takes place between one being and another the like of which can be found nowhere in nature.

Growth in a relationship is sometimes a complicated process of personal interaction, requiring an awakening to the forces within and an awareness of subtle nuances outside, in the words and ways of other people. The most inauthentic person can talk about the value of being authentic and can modulate his behavior to meet this external value. If authenticity is the rewarded attribute, the behavior of authenticity can be copied and carefully developed. But authenticity itself cannot be imitated, for it refers to the real perceptions and real feelings of the individual, not to calculated gestures, motions, and external behavior. It refers to meanings, not to words, to actualities, not to labels.

Being authentic is often a painful experience, because, along with joyful and peaceful moments, authenticity inevitably leads to conflict, anger, and dissension. In my own classes, I have known the terrible struggle involved in remaining genuine, true to my own self, while at the same time understanding and respecting the feelings of other persons. I have attempted to keep in touch with my own thoughts and convictions, to express what I believe to be true, while at the same time wanting to know the reality of the other person's perceptions and encouraging the other person to speak openly for himself. Not long ago, the impact of authentic confrontation was clearly felt in one of my groups. On this day I had come to share an exciting discovery, for me a moment of revelation and truth. From deep regions of myself, I spoke of the meaning of beauty, faith, and love, of the ultimate values that exist in every fundamental relationship and the belief that these values can be evoked, no matter how defeated or disillusioned a person may be. Somehow I felt particularly alive and filled with the desire to awaken in my students a thirst for inquiry and experience and a hunger for companionship and communion. But I was in one world and some of my students were in another. Jim remarked that I was engaging in speculation and fantasy. He made a series of nihilistic declarations, spoken softly and quietly and even with a gentle touch. In the process I felt myself being washed away in his declarative sentences. As he talked I felt a rising anger. "What's the matter?" I asked. "When were you burned to have such sour perceptions of human beings?" He told me he knew all about canned authenticity because he was often surrounded by it. As I interpreted his fallout, it had nothing to do with authenticity but was simply another form of alienation. Surely, I thought, he knew the difference between wearing a mask of honesty and being honest, between using words of authenticity and one's own real voice. Was he doubting my authenticity, or simply taking me into his meetings with others and showing me how the keen, shrewd eye for the weaknesses of people works, the eye trained not to see the truth but to look for underlying distortions? For me, he was exhibiting a facility for uncovering the meanness, hypocrisy, and cunning of others. I felt I was being put on by a cynical stance that, in itself, did much to create distrust and to arouse suspicion and guardedness. So I told him, in direct and pointed words, that his cynicism was, in itself, a reality that affected the situations he observed. He looked stunned and for several minutes simply stared blankly into space. Then, with a painful edge in his voice, he told me that I was not meeting him where he was at the moment, that my words were sharp and rejecting. He paused and added, "What you say of my cynicism is true, but you make it sound as if that's all there is to me!"

Now we were really at odds, we who had often expressed a common valuing of honesty and openness. It was this very dedication that was now creating the battle between us. I was learning how complicated a relationship is, how facets keep emerging that reveal new dimensions of the self, and how essential it is to stay with conflict and search for renewal in bonds with others. Once again, I was seeing how disturbing and strange and terrible a relationship can be.

To remain silent in the issue would simply initiate a pattern of pretense between us and begin to turn our meetings into clever games. As I saw it, Jim was making the beautiful into something ugly. But was it evil to speak of it? There was something in the soft-spoken, gentle way in which he expressed himself which irritated me, particularly when he was processing my words, altering them just slightly but overturning my meanings and making them appear as mere substitutes, which could be as readily simulated and exploited as any other meanings. But as he saw it, he was simply more in touch with reality. I could not meet him in that reality without denying my own self. I could not accept what felt like a twisting of my values into current coin of knowledge. I felt that, to maintain my own identity, I had to come up against him, openly and clearly, and let him feel my indignation at being misunderstood, at being received so shrewdly. I felt I had to let him know that he was turning me off with his more sophisticated experience. So I met him, true to my own experience of the moment; he felt the sting of my words. He said I was not accepting him as he was, that I was not accepting his perceptions. But to accept him I would have had to be dishonest with myself; I would have had to be receptive to a view of life and people that offered no constructive plan of action. My choice was between standing by him or by my own self; I could not confirm him in this conflict without violating myself.

After the strong current of feeling was expressed on both sides, we really began to listen to one another, each with his own voice, each with the integrity of his own experience. It was the first time we had met in conflict, and suddenly I realized that, until this encounter, we had never really known one another. Painful as it was, the experience had the ring of truth, the ring of some-

thing real. In the process of confrontation, neither of us
wavered in our concern for honesty; each remained true
to his own sights and senses. Within the anguish of
anger and pain we came through this meeting to a new
awareness of each other; a feeling of mutual appreciation and respect was ultimately achieved. In spite of the
misunderstanding and confusion, nowhere between us
was there a censoring voice. This quality of openness
in conflict, of staying with a reality of life as we perceived it, made our confrontation alive with meaning.
It is just this kind of vital issue that the authentic person
faces, for to tell the truth about one's own self, to share
with others one's real beliefs and interests and dreams,
is to risk oneself, to put oneself in a vulnerable position
for attack. When one shares the inner regions of himself, when one reveals his deepest feelings, convictions,
and experiences, he is actually trusting others; he is
offering true and vital dimensions of himself. And he
remains unfinished when he is not heard; he remains unfinished when he is not received. To restore this unity
of self with others, an open battle is sometimes essential. Ortega y Gasset remarks: "To be open to the other
is a passive thing. What is necessary is that, on the
basis of an opening, I shall act on him and he shall
respond or reciprocate to me. . . . The form 'we live'
very well expresses this new reality, the relation 'we'—
*unus et alter,* I and the other together do something and
in doing it *we* are."

The reality of human relations, the private worlds in
which each of us lives, the singular response of our own
senses, the strength of our ideas and feelings mean that
often we will not be in the world of the person who is
sharing and creating himself with us; we will not immerse ourselves in that person's perceptions and enable
him to move forward and beyond his present being;
rather, we are affected in such a way that we can only
respond in opposition to the other, consistent with our
own selves. When we are in conflict with others, we

may withdraw into sleepy states of boredom and indifference, or we may face the person in encounter. Both acceptance and confrontation are authentic ways, because they keep the persons together in reality, and as long as they remain together, whether harmoniously or antagonistically, genuine life continues; real facets of uniqueness and individuality are present, and the real identities of the persons are emerging. Thus, both conflict and affirmation can be forms of human caring, forms of trust, and ways in which the authentic person registers his existence in the world.

In the authentic relationship, each person stands by his own perceptions. The reality of these perceptions may be expressed through silent presence and affirmation; that is, through receiving the other person as he is, listening with one's total self and responding with appreciation and regard, thus enabling the person to feel human presence and concern and to become aware of himself. This process may lead the person to move forward to new dimensions of thought and feeling. The positive dialogue between the one person and the other may awaken new perceptions or deeper meanings and underlying integrations, or it may enable the person to see possibilities for further study or action. Harmony between self and other is one way in which growth of the self proceeds. However, growth is not always a harmonious and supportive experience. Sometimes the meeting of persons is a painful experience; sometimes the issues, the dissensions, are essential steps of forward movement. What is important is that the persons remain together, be who they are, and stand by their own perceptions. When people are together long enough, when each person is free to express himself—both the gentle and the angry feelings—there is a feeling of openness, there is an absence of censoring, and people actually learn to appreciate and care for one another. They actually learn to listen and to be in the dialogue, in the life, whether they are the center of the creation or not.

Growth of the self includes and requires interpersonal relations, meetings between I and Thou, in which each person recognizes the other as he is; each says what he means and means what he says; each values and contributes to the unfolding of the other without imposing or manipulating. And this always means some degree of distance and independence. It does not depend on one revealing to another everything that exists within, but requires only that the person be who he is, genuinely present. Actual fulfillment of a relation between men ultimately means recognition of otherness. Buber expresses this value in the following passage from *The Knowledge of Man:*

> When two men inform one another of their basically different views about an object, each aiming to convince the other of the rightness of his own way of looking at the matter, everything depends, so far as human life is concerned, on whether each thinks of the other as the one he is, whether each, that is, with all his desire to influence the other, nevertheless unreservedly accepts and confirms him in his being this man and in his being made in this particular way. The strictness and depth of human individuation, the elemental otherness of the other, is then not merely noted as the necessary starting point, but is affirmed from the one being to the other. The desire to influence the other then does not mean the effort to change the other, to inject one's own "rightness" into him; but it means the effort to let that which is recognized as right, as just, as true (and for that very reason must also be established there, in the substance of the other), through one's influence, take seed and grow in the form suited to individuation.

The truth is not learned by reinforcement and habit; it is learned by being in touch with one's own self and by being present to the other, by letting the inner reality contact the outer reality without filtering or censoring perception and awareness.

Thus these two components—man's yearning and hunger for contact with others and man's desire for solitude, privacy, and self-communion—are essential paths to growth and development of the person. Each process serves different human capacities and enables different human meanings to be actualized.

The third experience essential to man's fulfillment of himself involves the group, that is, three or more persons who come into meaningful interpersonal relations. The group contributes to self-fulfillment in a way that cannot be achieved by the person alone or in person-to-person meetings.

In the presence of widespread breakdown in human communication, distortion, hypocrisy, alienation, and violence and crime, a relatively new movement has emerged, a movement which Carl Rogers has called a potent new cultural development—the intensive group experience. This experience has been called the basic encounter group. Through my involvement with a number of these groups, I have come to see their potential significance as well as their potential danger. The basic encounter experience has been portrayed in movies, the most striking of which is *Who's Afraid of Virginia Woolf?;* in drama, *The Subject Was Roses;* in work with drug addicts, Synanon. It is now being used in church groups, in industries, in hospitals, in schools, with families, with all age groups. The encounter group is a small group, usually about twelve to fifteen members, and relatively unstructured. The group meets in intensive, continuous sessions, running from six hours to a week, often in a retreat setting. It chooses its own goals and directions. The focus is on immediate personal interaction. The leader is important in the initial moments in making orienting comments that provide a beginning structure; later he serves to facilitate the process or becomes a member, leaving the group leaderless.

Thomas describes the encounter group as follows: ". . . the props *are* removed and the individual is in a type of 'no exit' situation where he faces himself and others without benefit of the masks behind which he can ordinarily hide. . . . People become freer to express how they really feel toward each other. Generally, negative feelings soon occur. Irritations toward each other are expressed. Roles and game-playing are made more obvious to people and after a period of time their need to maintain them is lessened. Significant experiences are shared and gradually deep feelings between people emerge."

Rogers believes that the individual will gradually feel safe enough to drop his defenses and begin to relate directly on a feeling basis with other members of the group, that he will understand himself more accurately, will change in personal attitudes and behavior, and will subsequently relate more effectively to others in his everyday life situation. He believes, too, that the group will move from confusion, fractionation, and discontinuity to a climate of trust and coherence.

Two attitudes arise in the group that facilitate the process—an attitude of challenge in which negative feelings, irritations, and hostility are expressed, and an attitude of nurturance in which acceptance and love are expresed. Illustrations[2] of episodes involving each of these critical attitudes are taken from a recent unpublished study of Rogers. First, the hostile confrontation:

Norma: *(Loud sigh)* Well, I don't have any respect for you, Alice. *None!* *(pause)* There's about 100 things going through my mind I want to say to you, and *by God* I hope I get through 'em all! First of all if you wanted us to respect you, then why couldn't you respect *John's* feelings last night? *Why have you been on him today?* Hmm? Last night—couldn't *you*—*couldn't* you accept—*couldn't you* comprehend in any way at all that—that he felt his unworthiness in the service of God? *Couldn't you accept this,* or did you have to dig into it today to find

---

[2] Parts of these illustrations were included in Rogers, Carl R. "The Process of the Basic Encounter Group," in *Challenge of Humanistic Psychology,* James F. T. Bugental Ed.). New York: McGraw-Hill, 1967, and are used by permission of the author and publisher.

something *else there?* Hmm? I personally don't think
that John has any problems that *are any of your damn
business!* And as he's stated so many times, he's been
talking about various things—he doesn't understand
them and they're not clear to him so *why in the hell* do
you keep *digging at him?* Hm? Is it because of your
weakness? If *you're* the type—ooh—and his respect for
womanhood—he loves women—yes, he does, because
he's a *real person,* but you—*you're not a real woman*—
to me—and thank God, you're not my mother!!!!—'cause
my mother and I—and any real woman that I know
would not have acted as you have this week and particularly what you said this afternoon. That was so
crass!! It just made me want to puke, right there!!!!
And—I'm just shaking I'm so mad at you—I don't think
you've been real once this week! . . . And I'm so fed up
over "that nice sweet Norma," that nice sweet me—
"she's really participated this week just by smiling" and
"mhm, mhm mhm." Oh! I am *sick* and *tired* of this uh,
"Well, how do you feel?" and uh, "Can you tell us about
that?" "Well, did your brother-in-law have anything to
do with that when you were three years old?" And all
this *junk! Just—accept people for what they are—quit
trying to dig this jazz out of 'em. If the jazz is in there,
they'll bring it out themselves.* And, uh,—I—last night—
I felt so much—that John is a *real person* and I accepted
and understood what he was trying to say about his unworthiness, and this thing today about bringing in implications about his disliking *all* women—or his one image
of *the* woman, and his trying to have everything his way.
I just—I just don't understand why you try to read
these things into him because I—I just can't. And I just
think it's so *ugly* and if I—I'm so infuriated that *I want
to come over and beat the hell out of you!!!! I want to
slap you across the mouth so hard and*—oh, and you're
so, you're many years above me—and I respect age, and
I respect people who are older than me, *but I don't respect you, Alice. At all!* And I was so *hurt* and *confused* because you were making someone else feel *hurt*
and *confused* that if I left here—and I feel it right now
—and I don't care if it makes theory, sense, formula, to
any of you, but I hope it will to *you*—if I didn't say this
*to you tonight*—I'm just wondering *how many other
people you're going to hurt*—with this type of thing.
Outside in your everyday life—just not taking people for
what they are! *(A startled pause)*

An example of the nurturance attitude follows. Leo and Fred are speaking to Mary:

Leo: *(very softly and gently)* I've been struck with this ever since she talked about her waking in the night, that she has a very delicate sensitivity. *(turning to Mary and speaking almost caressingly)* And somehow I perceive— even looking at you or in your eyes—a very—almost like a gentle touch and from this gentle touch you can tell many—things—you sense in—this manner.

Fred: Leo, when you said that, that she has this kind of delicate sensitivity, I just felt, Lord yes! Look at her eyes.

Leo: M-hm.

The basic encounter group is an intensive, concentrated interpersonal experience. The ebb and flow of life brings with it strong feelings in relationship out of which an intimate community sense may evolve.

Perhaps I can best convey the nature of my experience with encounter groups by presenting, in modified form, a letter written after long hours of loneliness and solitude. The experience still seems alive and fresh within me and expresses what I currently see as the values and limits of encounter groups.

I have reached a sense of having struggled with an experience and perhaps have reached a point of clarification. I am satisfied that I have gone as far as I can for the time and am ready to move on to other ventures.

The center of my thinking these past two weeks has been the encounter group, reflecting upon my reading and especially my experience at Esalen Institute. Of what significance is the encounter group in evolving intimate human relations?

As I see it now, encounter groups have emerged and spread as a way of evolving direct, honest, pointed expression of feeling, sometimes strong, violent expressions of anger, resentment, and discontent. The purpose seems to be to face openly the forces of dissension, conflict, and general evil raging inside many people but rarely given opportunity for direct expression. The conviction is that straightforward, hostile tactics eventually lead to genuine, authentic transactions between persons, that direct attack and counterattack, in a climate where the basic intention is honesty of self-expression, will result in compassion and intimacy. The ultimate aim is the development of positive, loving, human relations. Though the beginning may be slow, awkward, and confused, soon the defenses are dropped and individuals confront one another directly with a range of emotions—anger, joy, sorrow, excitement, grief, tears, and laughter.

I see values in people meeting in groups for intense emotional confrontation, but I have reservations about certain aspects of the encounter group. First of all, I think it is a false assumption that people inevitably experience hatred and hostility when they are intimately involved with others. I do not believe that countering hatred and hostility with hatred and hostility always leads to an honest, healthy relationship even when the intentions are good. I also think that individuals engaged in combat must be fairly well matched or there is danger that the weaker opponent will be vanquished and destroyed. In any event, when the opponents are unbalanced, when the strong easily vanquish the weak, there is no real challenge, no real contest. Further, I do not believe that survival of the fittest is a healthy basis for human society (not even in an arena) though it may make sense in the jungle.

I believe it is possible for a person to meet hostility and hatred with pain and suffering, to absorb the blows and the sting of words, and through suffering to maintain his identity, his sensitivity, and to emerge from such a confrontation stronger. In other words, the encounter groups know how to use hostility as a force in authenticating life but have not recognized the restorative powers of pain and suffering. Whereas hostile exchange is seen as a step toward genuineness in communication, and thus as a good, pain is seen as corrosive and evil. Reception of hostility with pain is regarded as a deterrent to the deeper interpersonal process. This need not be so; in fact, it is not so in many interhuman conflicts. I think here of the secret agent in the movie The Ipcress File. He met the communist onslaught and brainwashing by maintaining touch with his own sense of pain. As the forces aimed at destroying his identity impinged upon him, he dug a nail deeply into the palm of his hand and through excruciating agony he withstood all the stimulations and pressures. He came out strong, alive and whole.

After all, isn't this what is at stake in encounter groups—the person's identity, however fragile or inadequate it may be? Somehow, with whatever strength, isn't this what must be maintained in the hostile exchange? And if it isn't, if the self capitulates in the face of group pressure, isn't it simply the substitution of an external set of definitions for one's own perceptions? If an individual, who is hanging on to a fragile identity, begins to believe what others say of him and substitutes their definitions of who he is for his own self-image, then is the "love" which may follow nothing more than approval and reward for submission and surrender? And in such an "encounter," who is being loved when there is no one to love? Isn't this what often happens to a child growing up in his family when parents begin to define who the child is and reinforce their definitions with rewards and approval? What else is the feedback of the group, or consensual validation, except the perceptions, reactions, and preferences of others? Ultimately, the person must define for himself who he is, the nature of his desires, feelings, and perceptions; and this he can do best in his moments of solitude and loneliness when he stands naked before himself; he must consider the opinions and perceptions of others from the vantage point of his own self and not be pulled into the collective stream, for the group is inclined to stand as a force against private, personal life, and it is easy to be pulled into the sweeping currents and whirlpools of the group. Solitude and loneliness are the only antidotes to strong group pressures. Feedback is helpful, but when self-awareness becomes a consensually validated matter, the individual is forced to retreat more and more from his own self. Only when feedback brings self-awareness which fits one's own experience does it enable the person to take the next step in his growth. "If real success is to attend the effort to bring a man to a definite position," says Kierkegaard, "one must first of all take pains to find HIM where he is and begin there. . . . the helper must first humble himself under him he would help, and therewith must understand that to help does not mean to be sovereign but to be servant, that to help does not mean to be ambitious but to be patient, that to help means to endure for the time being the imputation that

one is in the wrong and does not understand what the
other understands. . . . Instruction begins when you,
the teacher, learn from the learner, put yourself in his
place so that you may understand what he understands
and in the way he understands it."

I know from my own experience in the Esalen encounter group that I met Kris in a way that would not
have occurred otherwise. He was one person in the
group of whom I was only slightly aware until the basic
encounter meetings. But in all the critical and rejecting
comments he made to me that night and the next morning I did not feel hostile or rejecting in turn. Inside, I
was sweating, biting my mouth, cutting and hurting in
some pretty drastic ways. I received what he said and
even honored his right to say it, but in those moments I
felt entirely alone. We were in two different worlds,
facing each other but on very different paths, without
dialogue—subterranean or otherwise. I met Kris's hostility with pain and anguish. I absorbed it and inside me
for a while it was like a poison. But, at least, now he
was tangibly present and very real. Until those moments
of confrontation, he was another person, vague and un-
differentiated. But once we met head on and he condemned me as a detached intellectual, when he repeat-
edly blasted away at me, the pain I experienced enabled
me to stay with my own perceptions and not be carried
away by the sweeping attacks that did not fit my own
inner life. In the end, when all others were gone and I
walked without direction, not knowing where I was or
where I was going, but alone and lonely, Kris and I met
on the same path. We were traveling in different directions and I looked up and suddenly he was there. We
converged in that moment, our eyes met, and I felt
deeply his compassion. He embraced me and between
us there was no more horror; he wept painfully for long,
long minutes. And though I was overwhelmed at the
suddenness, extremeness, and totality of the moment, I
felt something deep inside—not just compassion, for I
experienced that with him many times that Saturday
night, but a human intimacy and depth, and tears of sadness and of joy, which washed away the darkness and
the gloom. Then quickly he was moving down a hill and
something warm and shiny and glistening beamed between us; I knew unexpectedly that we had shared a
moment of absolute communion. Then, only then, was

he wholly real to me—when we stood there on the same path and we were alone, person-to-person; it was unlike any moment with him in the group.

I believe in the value of transcendence. Many times in my life I have overcome obstacles to my own growth; I have discovered resources when none appeared available, and I have met many, many people who by all the facts which surrounded them should have been miserable, destructive, limited people but who, on the contrary, were vital, alive, wondrous, joyful people. Many times, too, I have felt emptiness, boredom, triviality, repetitiveness, sterility, and meaninglessness—but when I transcended the mood or feeling or situation, when I became involved, spontaneous and free, suddenly I was seeing with different eyes and hearing with different ears. This I could do only myself, in my own loneliness, when my life with others seemed futile. Who knows, who can tell what may happen next—waiting has its value in this and intention and belief, and then (it has no rational basis) boredom dissipates into interest, sadness into joy, emptiness into excitement. I think of Frankl's concentration camp victims. With all the brutality, cruelty, hatred, torture, disease, hunger, and cold, they still maintained their altruism, their love, sharing their last piece of bread, enduring terrible agony, handing over their last shred of clothing, freezing, but still serving the maimed, the dying, and the deteriorating people around them. Yes, I believe in transcendence of past, of environment, of pettiness, of shame, of hostility and hatred.

Finally, I believe, the encounter group ignores or violates a person's right to privacy. There are moments in a group when I want to be alone with my own thoughts and feelings, when I want to stay with my own inner process, struggle with my feelings—yes, and keep them to myself if this is my preference. When the group gets caught up in goals of self-disclosure, when it does not respect the person's decision to remain silent with reference to his own experience, when it does not recognize the value of private dialogue and silence in self-growth, then it creates barriers in communication and forces a pattern or process that is just as phony and just as much a strategy as the games and roles that people play in their associations with one another. Loneliness and solitude have an important function in group life; there are some matters that can be resolved in no other way. If these meditative, reflective processes are not recognized and respected, then the battles and conflicts which emerge rest not on the real issues between man and man but on false theories, false threats, and false assumptions. Kierkegaard wrote in one of his journals: "There is a view of life which conceives that where the crowd is, there also is the truth, and that in truth itself there is need of having the crowd on its side . . . a crowd in its very concept is the untruth, by reason of the fact that it renders the individual completely impenitent and irresponsible, or at least weakens his sense of responsibility by reducing it to a fraction. . . . No, when it is a question of a single individual man, then is the time to give expression to the truth by showing one's respect for what it is to be a man."

Perhaps what I have expressed here implies insurmountable objections to the encounter group and what it attempts to do. This is not the case. I see its value for some people, under controlled conditions. I think hostility does exist; I think it is affecting human relations and in its devious, hidden forms is killing genuine life. I think hostile confrontation can be the beginning of something honest and real between persons. I think it can lead to deep, genuine, loving experiences. This is what I have learned. This is what I have seen happening in some instances and I know it can happen in the face of gentler forces, in the presence of love, where the ultimate direction is one of compassion and goodness. I repeat, under certain conditions, within a certain climate, where the basic intentions are positive and underlying value is present, love can emerge. Then persons can know turbulence with one another, in challenge and contest, in struggle and encounter. At the same time, within the group there must be an unyielding trust in people, and a basic sympathy, and regard. I have learned from this that, for some people, *only* through combat can hostility be dissipated; only through countering hatred with hatred, openly, directly, clearly, and simply, can growth be achieved. I saw emerging guilt and anxiety which moved people to suffer, to atone, and to find love again, but now real love, genuine feeling in the one person for the other. Through violence and combat, through a battle in open, honest challenge, men can experience an eventual toughness and an essential caring for one another. Many questions remain.

Why must some people counter hatred with hatred in order to become genuinely involved? What happens in that single, solitary moment to bring about the radical shift from hostile criticism to compassion and love? It looks like such a turnabout of extremes—but is it? What are the conditions which facilitate the battle but keep the lines of attack, the opposing forces, enough in balance so that no one is overwhelmed, defeated, or totally crushed, so that at no point is there a point of no return, so that no one fails to get back up and face the ordeal? How can encounter groups recognize the value of privacy and not interfere with the individual's solitary moments, not impede self-awareness, which depends solely on the person's own struggles with himself? What kind of climate facilitates the exchange and keeps people together and the contest a verbal battle? And what underlying theme or value keeps alive the growth dimensions in these meetings when behaviorally and expressively destructive words and gestures, resentment, sarcasm, bitterness, meanness, and other forms of evil are central signs?

I know the encounter group has value in some situations with some people, but I'm searching for the kind of awareness that for me will make it a living reality, where all three structures are recognized and valued: solitude and loneliness, person-to-person dialogue, and intense group experience; then I can face both the solitary and the communal moments and know them in my blood and in my bones.

I think the encounter group represents a new perspective that may clear the way for many of us struggling for authentic life with others. But I also believe that the essential uniqueness, the elemental otherness of each person must be recognized and that moments of self-dialogue and private self-reflection must be respected in every human setting. The precept, "If you can't make it with people you can't make it," has a corollary: "If you can only make it with people, and not alone, you can't make it."

## REFERENCES

Bradford, Leland P., Gibb, Jack R., and Benne, Kenneth D. (Eds.). *T-Group Theory and Laboratory Method.* New York: John Wiley & Sons, Inc., 1964.

Buber, Martin. *Between Man and Man.* Tr. by Ronald Gregor Smith. Boston: Beacon Press, 1955.

Buber, Martin. *The Knowledge of Man,* Maurice Friedman (Ed.). New York: Harper & Row, 1967.

Frankl, Viktor E. *Man's Search for Meaning.* New York: Washington Square Press, 1963.

Greene, Maxine. *Existential Encounters for Teachers.* New York: Random House, 1967.

Kierkegaard, Soren. *The Journals.* New York: Harper Torchbooks, 1959.

Kierkegaard, Soren. *The Point of View for My Work as an Author.* New York: Harper Torchbooks, 1959.

Marcel, Gabriel. *The Mystery of Being,* Vol. I. Chicago: Henry Regnery, 1951.

Nietzsche, Friedrich. "Thus Spake Zarathustra," in *The Portable Nietzsche,* Walter Kaufman (Ed.). New York: Viking Press, 1954.

Ortega y Gasset, Jose. *Man and People.* New York: Norton Library, 1957.

Rogers, Carl R. "The Process of the Basic Encounter Group." Unpublished paper. Western Behavioral Sciences Institute, La Jolla, California, 1966.

Thomas, Hobart F. "The Encounter Group and Some of Its Implications for Education and Life." Unpublished paper. Sonoma State College, Rohnert Park, California, 1966.

CHAPTER 4

# *Sensitivity*

# *and*

# *Encounter*

To meet with a group of strangers and suddenly find oneself sharing private, personal concerns is a startling moment of reality In the hours of deep involvement and the quickening of inner life, persons are growing as individuals while at the same time becoming members of a genuinely caring group. From the depths of anger, rejection, and animosity, from the revealing of personal guilt and torture, out of the combined forces of group life, individuals meet honestly and confront one another with conflict and resentment as well as with tenderness and love. A way of life is created that makes other kinds of interaction pale, thin, and superficial. Pain, suffering, and anguish, when expressed, shared, and received, are just as much a unitive force in a group, just as much a restoring and strengthening bond as the ring of laughter and joy that pulls people together. To be an individual, awakening to unique and solitary feelings and at the same time deeply related to other human beings, to be authentically in touch with the one and the many, offers hope and optimism that man can live in the world as a universal being, can have real connections with communal life without losing contact with himself.

## THE INTENSIVE GROUP EXPERIENCE

Intimacy and depth of communication are generated in open, honest, intensive experiences, when individuals are willing to take the risks of an unknown journey, to share their immediate feelings, however strange or inexplicable, and to encounter one another directly, moment by moment. When individuals express their own convictions, beliefs, and feelings without defensiveness or facade, the usual, lengthy time commitments and complicated arrangements are not required. Self-awareness, intimate contact with others, and trust are created suddenly and quickly rather than in a gradual, cautious way.

Even the most hostile and destructive persons want to communicate with others, want to become constructively and genuinely related. The alienated person is suffering; alone, he is unable to face his own estrangement; but in a group, once the alienating thoughts, feelings, and mannerisms are out in the open, once they are met, recognized, and accepted or challenged, the individual begins to change; he moves in the direction of authentic presence, dialogue and encounter. The established patterns and habits do not continue, because the alienated self has been honestly shared, and in the sharing an explosion occurs that dissipates the old connections and facilitates new relationships. The alienated person no longer denies his alienation or hides from it; he permits others to see him as he is. In Rilke's poetic style: ". . . sickness is the means by which an organism frees itself of foreign matters; so one must just help it to be sick, to have its whole sickness and break out with it, for that is its progress."

When the individual breaks out into the open with his "sickness," he creates his own scene; he comes forward fully, clearly, and intensely, being who he is in the moment—in anger, sadness, doubt, sympathy, defeat, glory, in joy, laughter, and love. Each person owns himself, puts his cards on the table, and, in effect, declares: "Here I am. This is the nature of my existence." The negative side is expressed and, though it is not always welcomed, it is met and responded to. This may be risky or even dangerous in a group, for the passions of one member may tend to drown out other people; but the person who is willing to stay with a group and not withdraw or leave, not reject it by departure, will have his day, for the anxious or hostile man does not want to drag others into the pit with him, even though it may look that way. At bottom, each person wants to be rescued and helped out of his terror and deceit. It is not the uncensored, intense, powerful feelings coming through that bury and swamp others, but emotions coming piece by piece, from fragments of the person, going on and on and on. Fragmentation and compartmentalization strangle the person and produce grotesque relationships that sometimes look normal. The most violent of human dragons desires to be heard and accepted, wholly, in one huge moment. Even the most antagonistic and rejecting persons become gentle and valuing when others encounter them as human beings, when genuine bonds are developed. After the stormy explosions in a group, a glorious peace ensues, which brings with it a feeling of tenderness and communion, although the members of a group may have to live through long hours of almost unbearable pain and suffering and immense grappling with reality.

From my own experience, I have discovered that people learn to listen and care for one another; they learn to help one another grow; they become more sensitive, more alive, responsive, aware, understanding of self and others, more honest, and more gentle and loving. The most significant catalyst in this process is the willingness to share oneself with others—the doubts, the uncertainties, the conflicts and issues, the suffering and joy, the immediate feelings and perceptions—to share the most vital dimensions of being as they are emerging in oneself and in one's own relations with others, and the willingness, at times, to transcend one's own private individuality and reach toward a universal self and a universal meaning through communion with others.

Sharing is not a mere reporting of experience (past or present); it is a medium for opening into new relationships and, in the process, for developing insights and letting go. In sharing, a climate is created in which each person recognizes himself as he is, really notices each person within the group, and uses his senses in being present and in creating bonds with others. That which we know we come to trust; as each person shares himself in the personal, private world in which he lives, real knowledge is generated; a clarity of self and others is emerging. As each person finds a way to be with others, while growing both in his concern for himself and for others, a bridge of meaning is created. To share is to touch others with oneself, with the real feelings, burdens, joys, with whatever it is that represents the vital episodes of existence, the pain in having to live with misfortune and handicap, or the happiness of a new discovery or the ecstasy of a new relationship or a new love. When one shares the truly significant, whether it is enlarged in emphasis, value, or actuality, it nonetheless exists as a fundamental characteristic of one's self, and the direct, open sharing of it not only makes contact with the world of others but, when received and responded to, has an opportunity to change, to become clarified, to become consistent with the real. Thus, sharing is a way of being, a way to authentic relationship, an experience that immediately brings about a feeling of intimacy and provokes self-awareness and self-knowledge. It initiates a chain reaction; more and more people find themselves in a common world of interrelatedness.

What is it that prompts individuals to want to share the vital happenings? First, members of a real group come together in order to know themselves and others in a more significant way. Second, the leader assigned to the group helps to create an atmosphere for spontaneous expression, for open confrontation, for genuine involvement. Initially, through his perceptive, sensitive comments, his intuitive challenges, and his own presence as a sharing person, he encourages and sometimes directly invites others to speak and to relate immediate perceptions and feelings. Third, the individuals in a group are usually in an isolated setting and must depend on one another for companionship and support; they meet together for an uninterrupted number of hours (a day, a weekend, a week) and are away from the usual stimulations, habits, and associations. But, beyond these factors, what precisely triggers the crucial moment of sharing that in its deep, intense unfolding stirs people to union, and brings about a total group experience is a mystery. I believe that it follows no set pattern, that the critical moment is unexpected, that there are forces at work—intangible, incomprehensible, and inexplicable —that radically alter the way of life of people. In some of my groups, the critical moment occurred almost instantly and paved the way for individual searching, person-to-person dialogue and confrontation, and person-to-group involvements. In other groups, this moment did not occur until after many hours of intellectualizing, superficial observing and interpreting, and cautious maneuvering. And, in some of my groups, it did not occur until nearly the final hours when, at last, primarily through the tremendous emotional expression of one individual, a real group came into being. Here are some examples of significant sharing that precipitated intense group involvement, participation in depth, and a feeling of community.

## A Confrontation of Love

Twenty-four persons meeting for a two-day seminar in human relations had consistently remained with professional topics and questions during the first day.

Throughout the day I expressed my lack of interest and involvement in the topics and a growing feeling of boredom in listening to ideas and thoughts that I had heard many times before and that were much more cogently and fully covered in recent publications. Several times I remarked that the potential of the group for meaningful inquiry was being paralyzed by intellectual talk and wordy lectures and that life was being wasted. With these and other challenging criticisms, a force of resistance was growing against me and came out into the open: "You were invited here to help us develop as professional people, not to evaluate us as individuals." "When we heard you were coming, we thought you would tell us about your latest work, some of the new trends and techniques you are developing in counseling." "From your writing, I expected someone very different, someone more accepting and more patient." "When are you going to give us something we can use?" "How about a list of your most recent ideas?" These comments were made softly, but with sarcasm. I responded by saying that I was making an investment of myself and that I had anticipated a very different kind of experience. I would not travel two thousand miles just to summarize what had already been published or to talk away two days of my life. I had come to meet real persons—not just in a narrow, professional way but as whole human beings. What were they afraid of anyway? Why did intimacy frighten them? If our being together was significant, the new trends, techniques, and values in counseling would be experienced, lived right here and now, and not merely talked about and written down.

My outburst was followed by absolute silence; then came a series of questions, more thrown than raised, more in anger than curiosity. "What is Merrill-Palmer anyway? What do you do there? How do you run your own classes?" I did not answer these questions but expressed my belief that the group was evading responsibility for coming to terms with the real issues and problems that were dividing it. Now they were really angry with me. A verbal battle got under way that lasted about two hours. I was condemned as an outsider, as a person who did not belong, as someone who was trying to get them to bare their souls, to reveal themselves, nakedly, before others. I, in turn, said it was, of course, much safer to stay in one's own little corner of the world and not risk being hurt, not face the animosity and rejection, or reach out and confront others with the really painful happenings in human interaction—the ignoring, the slights, the failures to listen, the littleness, the hypocrisy and deceit. In just one day I had observed these dynamics, the neat cliques, the way when a person spoke only his coterie of friends listened, and even they rarely responded with any honesty or depth. As far as I was concerned this was no group at all; there was no real involvement, no struggle with mutual concerns. A number defended the group by stating that the academic year was coming to an end and that it was too painful to come close to people only to have to separate from them—that this was a time to start pulling away, to get ready for departure. They objected to my attempts to get them to reveal personal disputes and issues, to share their hopes, fears, struggles, resentments, the real loneliness each knew. By keeping a distance, by relating primarily on a professional basis, they hoped to pull up stakes without too much grief.

In character, this group was much like the groups I had met and worked with in the past. It was a congenial group, from which small units met and discussed classes, exams, assignments, papers, and experiences as counselors in school settings. But it was not a real group, where open, intimate encounter occurred, where the deep regions of the self and personal experiences were shared. On the surface everything looked normal, but since I had experienced the depth and meaning of intensive group life, I had become impatient with the fragmented values of professional groups—the cliques, the splits, the divisiveness, the status and hierarchical emblems, the basically unlived nature of that world, the lack of human meaning, excitement, and vitality in living. In this group the individual was not authentically and honestly met, known, and valued; the feeling was missing that one's existence really mattered. I believe that in each group—no matter how strange or familiar the individuals are to each other—there is a level of unity and integration that recognizes, includes, and values each single person, while at the same time reaching a universal, human principle that goes beyond the simple combining of individuals and makes for a genuine community. In each group there is a potential that requires the presence of each person as an individual, using his talents and resources to create personal meaning in living; but life in its deepest forms sometimes transcends the private self and stretches toward a cosmic or communal self. To actualize one's potential as an individual and as a member of a community is a complicated and exhausting challenge, but when this moment is achieved in a concrete encounter it is an incomparable experience of human meaning.

So I kept on struggling to stay alive, and this meant continually clashing with the group throughout the first day and the beginning of the next. Then I accepted as fact that these men and women were contented with the patterns they had established. I suggested that, if it were not too late, I would ignore my own conviction of what is of value in a group and would try to answer their questions.

An hour later I felt discouraged and depressed; I felt that I was playing the role of an expert; I felt unreal and alienated, and I said so: "Isn't there anyone who knows what I've been struggling for, who has any feeling for what it means in a human sense to live, to experience profoundly the value of being in a real group?" A long silence followed, then one person spoke: "Yes, I do. We don't have that kind of group here. Maybe we gave up early in the year. We're afraid to face our fears and resentments. All year I've wanted to have one real friend in this group, but there's no one I can actually approach and speak to straight from the heart. There are little clusters of people close to one another, but I'm not part of any of these cliques. I've been hurt by people in this group, but I've never let them know. I used to eat alone in the cafeteria, day after day, until one day I had enough courage to join some of you. When I did, I felt you tighten and silently you let me know I wasn't wanted. The only time I feel accepted is when I discuss safe, academic topics. None of you really know of the way I live or what I want in life but I guess none of you care. After weeks of futile effort, I decided to put on my professional mask and keep it there. *He* knows what I'm talking about; we're not a group; we haven't developed our potential as persons. We're supposed to be learning to be experts in counseling and in human relations; we know the right principles and procedures, but we aren't living by them."

This was expressed with an intensity of feeling, a force that was like a shock experience; the group was absolutely silenced. After a long pause, Pat, the major professor and supervisor, spoke in a choked voice, grappling with his feelings. He had not uttered a word until this moment. I could feel the urgency in his struggle and the difficulty he was experiencing in expressing himself. "Right now I'm just so mad at all of you and so hurt I don't know where to begin. I've been listening to you these many hours and you sound like we're all finished here; the whole scene is over; it's time to withdraw and become strangers again. You're the most important group of people I know; I've never felt so close, so in touch with you, as individuals, or been more honest. When you talk about making your exit two months in advance, that really hurts. That's like dying before you've fully lived. And . . . uh . . . right now

I feel . . . well . . . just . . . (choking, struggling, fighting back the tears) . . . Jim, I've known you half my life, half my life, and I've reached out to you in friendship again and again, and each time you've turned away from me. You've changed the meaning, you've asked questions, you've explained and explained, until my insides are aching from it, the pain, the rejection, the hurt. . . . Sometimes when I'm with you I feel sick. I want to shake you up, and . . . it . . . Oh God . . . it hurts . . . (Pat began weeping and covered his face momentarily; then he looked straight at Jim with tears streaming down his face.) It's so painful to want to reach you. . . . I really want to reach you . . . and it's so hard . . . because . . . because, Jim, I love you."

These words filled the room and created an atmosphere of human involvement and concern. But for Jim, the encounter was like the sounding of an alarm. What had happened to make this expression such a difficult, painful, and like-moving-a-mountain kind of reality? What had happened to make it necessary to break down thick walls and barriers for men to be comfortable and free with their feelings of tenderness and caring?

With the utterance of words of love, Jim moved away from Pat; Pat put his face in his hands, covering his tears and his anguish. Someone shouted painfully, "Jim, you've done it again. Can't you look at Pat—look at him and receive him? He just revealed his deepest feeling for you and you've turned him down." Jim did not respond to this plea; instead he asked me a question about whether a counselor should reveal personal feelings to his client. "No, Jim, I'm not going to permit you to use me to escape facing Pat." Jim looked from one person to another in the group but each message, though unspoken, was clear—an unwillingness to permit Jim to evade this moment of human meaning. After what seemed like a long, terrible struggle in Jim, he turned his body and face and eyes in Pat's direction. He was battling with his own feelings, and the tensions mounted inside. The words were difficult to form and difficult to speak, and Jim (a big, strapping football player) was involved in an inner struggle and challenge. "Pat . . . Pat . . . don't you know . . . I turned away . . . because . . . (and now the tears came streaming down his face) because . . . I can't quite believe anyone . . . could care about me . . . really love me . . . and . . . and . . . Pat . . . those are the most beautiful words anyone ever said to me." Pat lifted his face and he and Jim met—straight—with eyes glistening.

We all shared in this moment of human encounter, in this dialogue of love, and we were no longer strangers; we were a real group and we were alive, involved, caring, united. In the hours that followed, each of us came into being in a new way—openly facing the suppressed conflicts, the hidden grudges, and the painful moments of pride, shame, rejection. The individual masks were dropped; the resentments and irritations and hostile feelings were expressed. With each new struggle and confrontation, with each sharing, a new level of community developed. Though we were separate, we were one, and we kept this rich human meaning alive and moving until the final moment came, when none of us wanted to leave what we had created together. But we also knew that it had to end, so we let go, each in his own way, and we took with us a new dimension of individual identity and a feeling of communal richness.

## Disclosing Suppressed Resentments

Serving as a special consultant in a three-day seminar, I met with a group of professional persons enrolled in an advanced program in school psychology. From the beginning of this seminar, it became evident that there were barriers to genuine, interpersonal communication—distortions, defenses, contradictions, and hidden, devious messages. Although the guardedness of the group was apparent, there was also a willingness to work toward open communication. With encouragement from me, within a few hours challenging confrontations began to occur. In one of these, Marilyn was facing Stuart:

"What I want to know, Stuart, is why you dropped me after the first time we met. You were friendly and helpful when we first arrived, and I thought, 'Now there's a really nice guy, someone who cares about people.' Then suddenly I was turned off and out in the cold. If I hadn't liked you right from the start it wouldn't have hurt."

"I don't know what you are talking about. I never dropped you."

"Oh yes, you did. You have! Don't sit there and deny it. [Marilyn began to cry.] Many times I've approached you and . . . you don't even see me any more. I feel when I'm near you that, as far as you're concerned, I don't exist. [Angrily] You're not even looking at me now!"

The atmosphere in the room became tense and there was a feeling of suspension in the air. Bill, sitting next to Marilyn, became noticeably uncomfortable. He interrupted and asked if it weren't better for two people in conflict to settle their differences privately. He started to go on, and Jim cut him off in an angry, loud voice: "Will you shut up and let Marilyn and Stuart work this out! I'm fed up with you. For four weeks, now, practically from the day we arrived, you've disrupted every vital moment. When something significant is happening, can't you just listen? You manage to steer us into superficial directions every time. That says to me that you're afraid of your own feelings. You don't want to get involved and you're determined not to let anyone else. You're not calling the shots around here any more, because every time you do, I'm going to stop you and shut you up."

"That's the rudest thing anyone ever said to me. You have no business talking to me that way. You're lecturing me like a child."

"Maybe it sounded that way. Let's both shut up and let Marilyn and Stuart continue."

Marilyn had been weeping silently during this exchange. She looked directly at Stuart and spoke to him once more: "Why are you rejecting me?"

Stuart was really uncomfortable and fidgety now. "Maybe it's the other way around."

"No, it's not. I like you. I like you very much. Is it because of the age difference? You often lump all the young people together in our group and when you're talking, you generalize." (Long pause)

"I'm not relaxed with you anymore. When we first met I thought you were a stable gal. But that day when you were mad and were yelling at everybody I guess I got scared. You sounded like you were going completely to pieces. I expected you to have a nervous breakdown."

"I'm glad to know that you get scared too, Stuart, because I've had the feeling nothing bothered you. Whatever it was, you could handle it. You gave me the impression that you are a person who can be leaned on no matter what the problem."

"Maybe I'm afraid that someday you'll spill everything. You know, just spill your guts out, and I wouldn't know what to do with you. I'd be scared as hell." (Pause)

"Maybe, but I don't think that'll happen. (Long pause) Something else about me that you don't want to admit. Does anyone know what I'm searching for?"

The entire group, including Bill, was very much involved in this confrontation. A number of people spoke up, some directing their attention to Stuart and others to Marilyn. Some felt that Marilyn was too sensitive, that she was putting her own problems onto Stuart, that she wanted to cling and get attention, and that being critical of Stuart was a way of manipulating him. Others said that Marilyn was justified in her complaints, that Stuart tended to go all out in first meetings and then became diffident and cautious. A number of people described Stuart as a nice guy who didn't want to see anyone hurt; some described him as dishonest; others defended him as a straight person.

During the discussion Marilyn and Stuart were listening attentively. Then they faced one another again. Stuart was the first to speak.

"Marilyn, I didn't feel this way at first but I do now. I . . . uh . . . I guess I feel inferior to you. . . . you're smart in everything you do. You're glib—the words just roll off your tongue. Everything you say comes easily. In our classes, especially statistics, you're always right at the top . . . and . . . uh . . . when I'm with you I feel dumb. I'm scared I'm going to flunk statistics right now. What I don't need is someone around who spouts off like you do. I sweat in that course and plenty of times you've remarked how easy it is for you. If you were so sensitive, you'd stop telling me how able you are in statistics and you'd be more aware of what a struggle it is for me. Sometimes, when I'm with you, I get to wondering, 'What in the hell am I doing in grad school?' "

"I'd like to try to stop bragging and showing off. I really would, Stuart, because you're someone I'd like as a friend. Okay?"

"Okay!"

This sharing of personal resentment and animosity paved the way for the development of an intimate community. During the remaining time many personal experiences were shared: Lois, whose son had recently died and who had kept within herself the painful tragedy; Bob, who had just separated from his wife and who was living alone; Don, who felt he had been phony all his life, revealed the many lies he had been telling the group and his constant shame in being dishonest while training to be a school counselor; Lorene, who was losing control of her eye muscles and "was hiding" the growing disability. Others, not knowing, told her they had often become irritated with her because they noticed she looked away when they spoke to her. Many, many moments of tenderness and regard were shared. When the three-day seminar came to a close, there was a deep feeling of relatedness in the group; the faces of people were human, real. The hard lines had melted away, and suddenly, toward the end, I became aware of how beautiful people are when they are themselves—open, spontaneous, and free. Once more, I felt keenly the goodness of being with people when they are real—when they feel their sorrow, anger, joy, and love, when they learn to listen and trust one another. How much I came to appreciate being with this group and how fortunate I felt to be part of an honest community of human beings! Once again, I had seen and experienced the value of human involvement, the value of struggle with the negative and positive dimensions of life, and the miracle that happens when people are together—intimately, honestly—when they come to be sensitive and loving human beings. We came to a close, in a gentle way, humanly connected, and feeling that we had lived. We were all exhausted (from the day-and-night struggle and exertion), but we were exhilarated, and when we held hands as a group, I felt an uplifting joy. Everything in the world was bright and beautiful.

## The Clash Between Leaders

A kind of vibrancy filled the air as our first meeting got under way. Most of us plunged almost immediately into meaningful experience; we shared some of our most significant relations. But it was clear from the fidgeting, the whispering, and from the apparent lack of presence that not all of the seventy-five people were really involved. Following the initial hours of vital, alive exchange that encompassed most of the group, we began wandering around and shifting in and out of topics. There were long, awkward, embarrassing pauses. Having almost instantly reached a level of meaning and feeling that touched the majority of the group, having shared with those who were feeling keenly the desire to relate from the start, we were struggling to find a new direction. For several hours we continued in this frustrating and exhausting way with little progress toward genuine involvement, unity, and enrichment. Then, suddenly, the chairman of the department, who had not spoken at all during the day, pointed her remarks at me.

"You've been a real disappointment to me. I don't know what you expected of us, but I haven't gotten anything from you. From your writings, I wouldn't have thought you'd be such a demanding person . . . or . . . such a performer. You've put on quite a demonstration, but I don't feel anything real coming from you."

"Welcome to the group! I wondered if you were just going to sit back while the rest of us struggled to create something real, or if you'd put your own feelings on the line. I've wondered what was happening with you—now I know."

"That's just as phony as the other stuff you've been putting out."

"How would you know? You haven't really been here most of the time. You've had your antennae out in all directions scanning the horizon to see what's going on. What do you know of the real in me or the phony? You haven't given yourself to any situation that has arisen here."

"I've given enough of myself to recognize a show when I see it. You're not at all what I expected. I never thought that Clark Moustakas would be demanding, impatient, and pushing, but that's all I see in you now."

"That really hurts—that that's all you've seen in me for two days!"

"There you go again. I don't feel any hurt coming from you. I don't feel any of the things you say you're feeling."

"No, you don't because you're not hurting. You're not listening to me. And right now I'm angry as well as hurt. If I screamed and yelled at you, if I cursed you, then you'd know my feelings. But you can't see my heart pounding or the quickening of my breathing, and you can't hear the sharper tones in my voice. From the moment I arrived for this seminar, I've had the feeling from you that I was a piece of property to be attended to in due course. Even in the initial introduction, I got a stylized response, and while shaking my hand, you were already looking to the next person being introduced. You've been a perfect hostess and administrator, but where are you? Who are you? Talk about playing roles —you're a real pro!"

"That was a nice speech but you don't know what you're talking about."

During this exchange, the tension in the group mounted. People had become increasingly uncomfortable but somehow had managed to remain silent. Then the outburst came.

"I'm not going to sit here and listen while you two wash out your dirty professional linen."

"I've heard enough. If this is some kind of private grudge, you can fight it out some other time, in some other place."

"I feel we're being used. I resent very much being exploited. I don't intend to be their therapist."

"I'm really very uncomfortable listening to this. I can't take any more of it."

"I think we should all leave and let them work it out. If we leave them alone they can settle this dispute themselves."

One by one the group walked out. I wanted to call out to stop them, to say that this was an issue for all of us, but I was held back by the thought that in the light of what had been said, such an effort on my part would be viewed as one more staging maneuver. Eleanore and I faced one another, but after a few moments of uncomfortable, painful silence she looked at her watch and left, saying she had another appointment. In this group I had once felt hospitality and warmth, but now I felt absolutely desolate and lonely. I had a strong desire to go back to my room, pack up, and pull out. This state of depression lasted throughout the night. Restless, moody, and sleepless, I watched the sun rise. I re-examined the happenings of the previous day many times and each time came to the same conclusion: For a while it had been good; many of us were humanly connected, but by the end of the day this feeling was completely shattered; the whole situation had fallen apart, and I was extremely pessimistic that any value would come from our final day together. I walked on the campus and noticed the different kinds of flowers, growing quietly and peacefully. It seemed that everything I saw was naturally related and that only people found the making of genuine ties a terrible struggle. I was weary of furious words, of misunderstandings, of rejection, suspicion, and distrust. I just wanted to be quiet and peaceful, too. But I felt alienated and sick, and wished simply to continue to be alone. Each time I considered the problem, I saw no way of resolving it. In my numerous experiences in groups, I had been characterized in many negative ways over the past two years—detached, intellectualizing, uninvolved, manipulating, unfeeling, impatient, weak and ineffectual, pushing, and passive; but I had never been told I was unreal and phony. I reconsidered my presence in the group from the moment of my arrival. The memory returned, a feeling of being strangely elated and euphoric on that first morning. I had been caught in a heavy rainfall and was thoroughly drenched. At first, I tried to escape the rain, until I realized that I was running because everyone around me was running. I started laughing. What was this rain really like? I wanted to know. So I just let it fall on me. I welcomed the rain, standing in the open, feeling the rain against my body and my face. I noticed the greenness of the grass; it seemed that each blade was reaching up to greet the falling water. I no-

ticed the wind blowing the trees, like the rhythm of a
new dance amidst a glorious shower. I listened to the
singing of the birds; each sound was distinct and beautiful and clear. All at once I was immensely happy; I
was vibrating and tingling with strange sensations; I was
absolutely entranced! My body responded with fresh
movement, and suddenly I was singing and dancing in
the rain. Completely wet and in a glorious mood, I arrived for the first day of the seminar. In this uplifted
spirit, I spoke spontaneously of the wonderful avenues
of sensory awareness and expression, the limitless feeling of touch, of being aware of the meaning of touch
and of knowing and relating through touch; I spoke of
what it was like to know, actually know, the feel of rain.
Suddenly I broke out; I wanted to touch everyone and
I did—handshakes, embraces, dancing movements, and
many other kinds of gestures. When I looked back on
this ecstatic beginning, I could see how it might be regarded as staged and unauthentic. But I had felt wildly
alive and caring; of this I was certain. I was swept
along by vibrant rhythmical forces—feelings that had to
run a full course. Many people in the group had come to
life with me, sharing deep personal experiences, relating encounters in the woods and mountains and by the
seashore. A number had spoken of the difficulty of
touching, of forbidden childhood experiences, of current
relationships where touching was threatening and disturbing; even in marriage, spontaneous touching was
often denied. Thus, many, probably most, of the persons in the group had opened themselves to sensory expression and were noticing the exquisite nature of real
life. Although the entire group was not involved, I felt
heartened by our experience; I felt a growing intimacy
and an optimism that we were moving toward the development of a community. Now the whole scene had
changed.

As much as I dreaded beginning again, with all my
doubts that anything constructive could happen, I joined

the group at the scheduled time and opened the meeting.

"I want to begin by relating how I am feeling right now. I spent a hard, restless, soul-searching night. And at the moment I'm feeling, well, unusually raw and sensitive. I have a strong desire to be away from here, to be home, anywhere, with people who know me. Yesterday afternoon I felt that you walked out on me. What happened between Eleanore and me happened in this group; our conflict grew out of these meetings, and, as I see it, you were all involved. We needed you to get to the root of our feelings and you needed us to bring some meaning into what was rapidly becoming a dull gathering. When the going got rough, when it looked as though you might have to take a stand, you walked out. I was left to struggle, completely alone, with what was happening. I started feeling sorry for myself, maybe, and feeling, too, that if you were going to reject me, I might as well walk out, too. In every group there are bound to be setbacks and severe trials among individuals. I know from my own experience that sometimes it is necessary to undergo a period of angry conflict, but that out of these hard, painful moments deeper, more honest experiences in human relations are created. Apparently some of you are happy with the comfortable, easy moments, but where you are most challenged you'd just as soon withdraw. I've had some rough moments before in a group, but I've never had an entire group walk out on me. So I guess what I'm saying is that if you feel you've had enough we can quit right now and each of us can go his own way."

Eleanore whose presence I had felt completely while I was speaking, responded immediately:

"I certainly don't want to quit. I had a hard night too. In the middle of the night I went for a long, long walk and spent much of the night in the woods—thinking. I want to tell you, Clark, that I have been unjust to you. I had an image of you before you came, and I kept looking for that image, so I never really saw you as you are.

I could not accept you because I expected someone else. And that's it, the problem is with me; I had an advance picture which is very different from what I've seen. And . . . well . . . I'm terribly sorry about it. But I've dispensed with that image this morning and I feel fresh. I don't want you to be other than you are and I really am ready to meet you. I'd like to spend the day with you."

"What you're saying just . . . well . . . I'm feeling so thrilled all over and loving toward you. I just want to . . . well . . . if you don't object . . . I just have a strong desire to hold you near because . . . because . . . I feel deeply your presence and it just isn't enough to put this feeling into words."

At this point I walked across the room where Eleanore was sitting. She stood up and we embraced and whispered quietly together. I felt like singing; the gloom had been broken and I felt really good again, really happy to be with people.

From this point, each person spoke from the depths of his own life; numerous confrontations were opened and people who had been closed to each other were facing feelings, issues, problems; increasingly, a community was being formed and new identities were emerging. We closed with several minutes of silent meditation, and then we sang happily together. Again, the unexpected had happened; out of a powerful confrontation, and the clarification and resolution that had come from it, we re-emerged as a real group.

## The Challenge of Sister Ann

We were nearing the end of an intimate, intensive group experience that had evolved over a period of three days, when Sister Ann faced me with a sincere and pleading but angry voice. The words came in a flurry.

"I've been mad at you almost from the moment you first arrived, and if I don't say this now I won't be able to live with myself. I spent the night searching within my soul for a way to speak to you. I've been afraid to talk because I have such a strong reaction to you; I don't know what will come. When I think of what you've been doing here I get choked up and I'm afraid I'm losing control. Last night I talked with two priests and, yes (pause), well, *I'm really mad at you! I* don't understand you—your voice has real feeling in it—gentle, sensitive—and your eyes but . . . but . . . I've got to ask you this and I want a straight answer. I don't want you throwing it back to me because . . . well . . . because I've got to know. Everything I'm going to say depends on this. I've got to know. *Do you believe in God? Do you pray?*"

I didn't know what to say. I knew this was a crucial moment between us and for the group. But I honestly didn't know how to answer Sister Ann in a way that would reflect my own convictions and experiences while at the same time communicating in Sister Ann's language.

"My hesitation is that I'm trying to find words to convey my own feelings. (*Pause*) I believe that there is a force in life which is beyond me, a cosmic power at work, which exists in the real world, a mystical power which I cannot describe but which I have felt—in times of great joy and happiness and in moments of desperation and misery . . . a sense of wonder, too, which I feel in the grandeur of nature. I have felt the presence of some universal, intangible value, yes, I could label this God, which has restored me as a human being. When I have faced disease, tragedy, death, I have known a spiritual presence which enabled me to be redeemed, to go on living when I felt like dying, to return to human existence when I wanted to remove myself from it, to face my enemy, with compassion, and to return to people I have forsaken."

Sister Ann began to cry, painfully, for long, long minutes. She lowered her head and turned herself away from me but then she looked up, in my direction, facing me.

"No! No! I mean a personal God, in the image of man. Not one you can touch but one whose presence you feel. How can you live without that? I can't! Life would have no meaning at all if I stopped believing in God—a personal God, a perfect being, who suffered and is suffering for our sins, and who can bring peace and eternal salvation to man. You are a good man. I feel *that* from you but I'm confused because . . . because . . . well, if you don't believe in God as a supreme being then I must doubt everything you say. You will never convince me."

"Sister Ann, I understand, but I can only speak directly from my own experience. I know the supreme feeling of coming out of the depths of despair and loneliness, the surpassing moment of departure from suffering—and suddenly I am in touch with life. I know the feeling of coming close to spiritual death, of aching and knowing that something in the depths of me, and in the depths of life, is at war or is dying; I know the feeling of glory in stepping out of the black pit and seeing, as if for the first time, the movement of the trees, the feel of the wind, a blade of grass, a flower, a human face. Whatever it is that creates this existence—all of life, all of being and nonbeing too—whatever it is, it is beyond tangible realities; it is supreme in being. I experience many moments, most moments, as a desire to chant words of appreciation, words of gratitude, ways to recognize and honor the triumph of life and of being, a desire to sing prayers of joy and exultation."

"Prayers of joy and exultation? But what about prayers for redemption and salvation? I pray to God, *to God,* many, many times every day to help me to become a better human being, to guide me in the right directions, to help me to help others in distress, and to forgive me for my weaknesses and my mistakes and my imperfec-

tions. My prayers give me strength and help me to go
on living and to find a purpose and a meaning in living.
(*Pause*) *Do you pray?*"

"Not in the sense of repeating printed prayers, or bib-
lical prayers, but . . . in a way . . . the chants I create
are spontaneous words of great sorrow and misery and
a search in mourning for some answer, or they are words
of gratitude for the wild happiness and ecstasy of some
peak moment. No space but that as vast as the limitless,
infinite space of the universe can contain the magnitude
and immensity of these feelings."

"I will not thank you or anyone else here for what's
happened these past three days, for the deep feelings we
have shared together. Our growth as individuals and as
a group is not your doing. It is God's and we should all
be grateful for what he has brought to us and given us."

"And what about the unfinished issues, the broken
bonds, the diminishing moments that we have also experienced here? Shall we give thanks to God for those
too?"

Sister Ann was crying very hard now and through her
tears she shouted at me:

"Yes. Yes. There is a reason for those experiences
too . . . there must be . . . there just is . . . because
if there weren't then I'd have nothing to live for . . .
nothing at all. . . . When I was a very young child my
mother died suddenly. And I loved her more than anyone else on earth. Then all at once she didn't exist anymore. And, oh, how I have missed her! I remember my
father weeping over her dead body; and, hanging on to
her, he cursed God for taking her life. I grew up without
a mother—yearning, suffering, watching other children
with their mothers. Without her, my life was empty;
only one thought kept me alive, that one day I would
join her in heaven—if I lived a good Christian life as she
did. To this moment I treasure the memory of my
mother and I know that we will be united. I want to
take my final vows to prepare for the eternal life after

death. Don't you understand what I'm saying? Don't you know what it means? (*Pause*) I know I've lost control. I'm emotional, but this is deeply upsetting me and confusing me."

"Sister Ann, do you sometimes doubt that you have made the right decision? The way you are trying to convince me may mean that you are also trying to convince yourself."

Sister Ann screamed in pain and cried for several minutes.

"Oh yes, many, many times. Whenever I see babies who look like me, I think of my own unborn children, and the fact that I'll never be a mother. I become very sad; I begin to doubt that I should take my final vows. There are other times, confused and uncertain, that I pray very hard for a sign to the right path. I'm young and I have many strong emotions. I feel passionate about so many things. But is it my youth? Or is it an essential weakness and a basic doubt? In these past two days I find myself defending God and His place here. Such experiences convince me that I am a believer, but I know I have difficulties to overcome. (*Long pause*) I thank God, but I also thank all of us for these days of honesty and fellowship."

Sister Ann was now smiling serenely, and a gentle peace had settled in the group. There was a feeling among us of unusual intimacy and worth. Someone put this meaning into words. We sat quietly a few more minutes, and before closing someone suggested that we pray together. It was a glorious feeling—to be in a real community again.

## The Spontaneous Love-In

Although the face-to-face confrontation, the open, direct disputes and battles between persons are often the breakthrough toward the creation of meaning and value, I know from my own experience that it is possible for people to come together for the first time and to be in immediate harmony. It is possible for strangers to develop an almost instantaneous warmth and to experience a feeling of mutuality and relationship, for the powers and capacities in a group to work toward evoking intimate feelings, without any need for angry conflict and battle, without any need for defenses and barriers. Recently, with twenty-five other persons I experienced, within a few hours, a compelling, intense, total feeling of community.

Our group met daily for a week, and each person shared the critical situations he was facing: what it means to love a child, the preciousness of time and the absolute significance of being aware, being in touch with a child in a unique relationship, not letting the days just pass but getting involved with a child in significant activities—talking, walking, listening, playing, entering the child's world and participating with depth, imagination, enchantment; what it means to love one's wife, the way in which love in marriage is expressed, the significance of music, art, poetry, and even flowers and nature in the development of love.

With surprising rapidity, each person was available to the other. When one individual was struggling painfully to share an extremely difficult, almost unbearable experience, every person in the group was there in that person's world, listening, supporting, gently encouraging. These individuals related, with deep feelings of anguish, sharp rejections by their families; the death of a friend, in which the person felt some responsibility; the killing of a child in an automobile accident; the humiliation and shame connected with an impending divorce; the terribleness of self-denial and maternal manipulation and domination; the struggle to restore a broken relationship; and problems connected with alcoholism and drugs. Each person was currently living the experience, not merely describing, but vitally sharing moments of grief and suffering and sometimes joy and happiness. One young lady shared her experience with

her father. Their relationship was an almost totally rejecting one until he was near death from a severe heart
attack. She visited him in the hospital and vowed that,
if he recovered, if she had "a second chance," she would
openly disclose her feelings of estrangement from him
and her desire to have a truly good relationship with
him. The moment of confrontation, the challenge of
love, occurred when he left the hospital. Each revealed
to the other dark, hidden resentments and bitter feelings; each related the incidents that created them. From
these daily sessions a new feeling was developing between them. Now, in our group, she was urging others
to be aware of the brevity of life, of the quick passing of
every relationship, and of the necessity to restore a
healthy pattern of living with parents, siblings, and
others. Each of us became more pointedly aware of ourselves, of our own human presence to one another, and
the feeling of intimacy and caring was deepened.

It is not possible to recreate all the significant moments in this group, but each person shared deep roots
of himself. And in the expression, in the sharing, we
were being humanly connected—until the flow of life
among us was rich with warm, beautiful feelings.

In one of these episodes, Martha related the painful-
ness of being in love with a married man and of knowing that this love could never be openly acknowledged
but would always be secretive and lived behind the
scenes, in shadows. She traced this relationship from
the beginning, its gradual unfolding, and its peak moments. She spoke of her early years of rejection and
feelings of inferiority, of all the big events in high school
and college in which she did not participate because
no boy invited her, of how, on graduation day, her
parents gave her the first corsage she had received and
her feeling of not wanting to hurt them but also of not
wanting to wear flowers that had been given out of pity
and not out of love. She shared the moment when the
man she loved, from his own spontaneous feeling,

brought her flowers and the deep meaning this moment had for her. It is too much to be able to create, but Martha was actually unfolding as a self with us, and in that emergence we felt close to her; we saw the inner light and the depth of human love that was Martha, and in the seeing we were all enriched as human beings. We embraced the tragedy of an unfulfilled relationship, while at the same time deepening our own relationship to Martha and as a group.

The almost spontaneous sharing of the big events in life, the joys and the tragedies, the conditions in which each person lived, the immediate, present feelings of self, the vital moments with others and the sharing of feelings within the group, in poetry, in dialogue, in total group activity—all of these aroused feelings that made life colorful, vivid, alive with meaning. It was a completely gentle process, and the tenderness just kept growing until our hours together contained such an involvement and dedication that we came to be known as a "love-in" group. It was an experience I will always remember because of its completely positive nature. From it I discovered that people can live together peacefully, in a completely accepting and loving way, and still be direct and honest and still achieve depth in relationships. I discovered that a genuine community can develop without denying or minimizing spontaneous individuality.

## The Breakthrough in a Group

In one of my groups, we had struggled for almost two days without any significant development. There were many splinters and fragments of life and a few moments when we were united, but there was a strong sense of egoism pervading the group, a self-centeredness that had an excluding character so that a number of individuals were cut off. It was a discouraging experience to see life being wasted on mere verbalizations and to see people exclusively concerned about their own private situations—to see people stagnating, repeating themselves, unwilling to be open to themselves, to others, to new life. I expressed my disenchantment with myself in the group and appealed for someone to share some really fundamental experience, to share some vital episode that really encompassed life, some feeling that totally embraced the person; I urged that we all drop our social masks and be who we are.

A long period of silence followed. Then one person spoke painfully of the ending of a crucial relationship, of his feeling that he would never again know intimate moments of sharing and of being with this person. He spoke too of the fact that teaching children and becoming significantly related to children had given a meaning to his life. In his hour of deepest alienation and despair, children had enabled him to feel once more a connection to the human world, a feeling of value in watching their creative potentials emerge and unfold in art, music, literature, in science, in imagination, and in play, and of the precious nature of contributing to growth.

The entire group felt the depth of his mourning and the personal meaning in the sharing. In every dimension of my being I felt his suffering, as thoroughly and completely as any moment in my life. His words had touched me in the depth of my heart, and in agony I cried out my neglect of my own children who had been so physically near during the past three weeks of seminars and workshops and yet from whom I had been far away. I had been so totally immersed with others that I had barely noticed them. Suddenly, in that moment, the entire vision of it flashed through me and I became painfully aware of each of them. I knew from my knowing of them that in many ways they must have felt our separation, as I did—two thousand miles away from home, cut off from friends, isolated in a strange place, living in crowded conditions, not even having the solace that comes from the privacy of intimate family living. It was a painful awakening, and I resolved that as soon as we completed the session I would find my children and somehow let them know that I really wanted to be with them . . . just give myself completely to happy, exciting activities with them.

Many persons in the group spoke of their relations with children—at home and in school. Words and feelings were awakened in all of us of the treasures of living with children and of a realization of ultimate value in sharing experiences with them, in opening opportunities and resources to them from which a good life could be created. Among the many keen and piercing episodes was the agony of Yetta's experiences in her final practice-teaching assignment.

"When you speak of children as real people, as precious, creative individuals, that really hits me, because sometimes I hate myself and I hate what I'm doing—what's happened to our schools anyway! I've been teaching in a school where I'm forced to march children in unison, where I'm forced to silence and suppress all their natural impulses for expression, all their spontaneity and exuberance . . . and every time I do my insides rebel and I am sick . . . sick of the whole thing. We don't have schools in this country; we have institutions for maiming children, killing their interests and desires and taking away anything that brings meaning, life, happiness . . . oh . . . whatever made me think I wanted to be a teacher anyway! I can't stand any more of it . . . I just can't continue doing what I'm doing with children and have any peace of mind. I want to create, not destroy, and I know I am destroying when I see the naturally expressive faces and bodies of young children move like machines. Perhaps I should just realize that I am not made to be a teacher who forces children to fit into a system of rules and practices that are damaging. Or should I stay and see if I can live with it while doing what I can to make the school a human place for learning. It has taken me all these years to get a degree and a teaching certificate. I can't do what I'm doing to children any longer. I have always wanted to be a teacher; I've always been excited about the idea; I never thought that schools were so regimented, that teachers became hardened and that children were miserable."

Yetta was supported by members of the group who pointed out that her sensitivity and caring were certain to bring a humanity to the school if she could only be herself and not submit to the system. Other teachers in the group explained that they, too, had been through the horrors of practice teaching in a rigid school but that, as independent and autonomous teachers, they were free to close the door of the classroom and create an atmosphere that encouraged and enabled individual growth and genuine group life. Many people spoke with Yetta and, in the dialogues, a warm glow of human life was emerging. The sharing continued into the late hours; in the process we became a real group and continued in this way until the hour of departure.

## Concluding Comments

Although common incidents and experiences have occurred in the groups in which I have participated, one thing is certain—each group is unique and different. No set of dynamics or procedures or techniques can fully characterize the development of a group when the members are open to what actually is present in each of the persons and in the whole. Further, I am convinced that it is not the confrontation as such but the sharing of one's life with others; the sharing of one's feelings with reference to oneself and others in the group, and with reference to significant persons in one's world; the sharing of ideas, convictions, values, abilities, feelings, whatever it is that constitutes one's presence as an individual and as a person in the group, the alienating and the relational conditions and events. Sharing is the key to intimacy—open, honest, direct, unqualified sharing. I am also convinced that the anguish, the pain, and the suffering that human beings experience and share with others are more integrating, uniting, and connecting emotions in the creation of community life than are the angry encounters and disputes—though it may be necessary to unleash the hostile side before the painful feelings of isolation, loneliness, rejection, terror, and inferiority can be expressed and shared. Kahlil Gibran once wrote: "You may forget the one with whom you have laughed, but never the one with whom you have wept." I would add, "You may forget the one with whom you have fought, but never the one with whom you have suffered."

## SENSITIVITY APPROACHES AND TECHNIQUES

Sometimes, in creating a climate of openness and freedom, I have found it helpful to employ one or more of the sensory awareness techniques or "encounter" methods. These approaches are not used to replace the face-to-face confrontations, the intense verbal exchanges, or the meaningful sharing among individuals, but they are of real value as catalysts or as initiators of significant happenings in a group. I do not know which persons are responsible for originating specific sensory awareness and encounter methods, but most of them I first saw employed by the staff and consultants of Esalen Institute. My application of these methods reflects improvisation and variation based on my own experience.

### The Trust Experience

In a recent group scheduled for a three-hour seminar, we used nearly an hour labeling ourselves with names, occupations, residences, and marital status and talking about the difficulties in getting started in a meaningful way. This was followed by long pauses and uncomfortable silences. Increasingly, I became aware of a physical tension in myself and others. Each of us seemed to be waiting for someone else to begin; there was an obvious reluctance to get into anything vital or real. I asked the members of the group to join me in an activity that might help us relax and promote a feeling of openness and trust. I indicated that sometimes, through physical encounter, through touch, a feeling of relatedness can be quickly developed.

The group formed a circle. One person stood in the center of the circle, closed his eyes, and fell forward, backward, or to the left or right. To the extent that the person was relaxed and trusting he would fall without buckling his knees or holding back. In starting, the person in the center chose which way to fall, but after the original fall the members of the group pushed the person in whatever direction they decided. Sometimes this was done by one person and sometimes by several people pushing at once. The person in the center decided when to pull out and join the circle. In our group it became increasingly spontaneous as each person took his place in the center. The activity became more relaxed and free; there was much laughter. For some, it was initially frightening, but the physical contact, being pushed and falling in different directions, promoted a feeling of confidence, and the person in the center (and some members of our group were over sixty) increasingly fell with trust. These physical encounters had broken through the tension and stiffness, and when we sat together again we were relaxed and ready to begin. The change in the atmosphere was obvious. One person in the group began almost immediately to relate a betrayal in the family—to share with us the shock of suddenly discovering (the previous evening) that both of her teen-age sons had been taking marijuana and LSD for several months. The drug itself was extremely threatening to her, but the knowledge that her sons had deceived her tossed into doubt her entire relationship with them. It was this doubt and her own sense of failure and inadequacy that constituted her essential struggle in the group. Out of this struggle, she began to see some concrete ways of approaching her sons and coming into a new relationship with them. This kind of personal sharing continued to the end of our time together, when each of us felt that we had experienced meaningful life in a group.

An approach similar to this, and perhaps less threatening, which also promotes a feeling of physical relaxation and trust (without the degree of risk or danger), also involves the forming of a circle, with one person standing inside the circle. The individual closes his eyes and is then passed to each person in the circle until he reaches his starting point. Each person in the group navigates the circle, being pushed and pulled by the members of the group. As the person is passed around the circle, he may be turned around; he may "fall" or be pushed or pulled from one person to the next; he may be held and momentarily embraced; there are numerous possibilities. Each group improvises the specific ways in which the method is carried out, reflecting the particular individuals involved. As the spontaneity of the group increases, as a sense of abandonment occurs, new ways of encountering and a feeling of relaxation and euphoria are created. The whole experience becomes increasingly unique, exciting, and unpredictable. Part of the challenge of the group is to discover its own particular way and to vary and improvise, to evolve an experience of increasing freedom and increasing joy.

For some, being touched and having physical contact with a group of strangers is frightening. Touching among adults is ordinarily forbidden in our society, except under appropriately defined conditions with appropriately labeled persons (usually relatives). It is quite a revelation—the feeling of being touched and of touching many other human beings! An awakening of human feeling occurs and an awareness of oneself that quickly dissipates the false stiffness and the bodily rigidity that are defenses against genuine being and genuine relationship.

In both of these "touch and trust" approaches, the size of the group should be limited to eight or ten people. If the original group is larger, it should be divided into smaller units. The group must be large enough to accommodate the falling person but not so large that each member is not in direct physical contact with every other member.

Another feature of the sensitivity approaches is that, at some point, each person is the center of the experience, the central figure in life with others. For many this in itself is a rare experience—the attention, the focus, and the self-awareness that are engendered.

## The Cradle Experience or the Crib Technique

For this approach, two parallel lines of people are formed. One member of the group is lifted and lies outstretched in the arms of the other members. Each person is in touch with the one being held. Positions may be changed during the experience. The person closes his eyes and is rocked from side to side or up and down or forward and backward. The person's head is held and his arms may be crossed or dangle freely beside the "crib." A feeling of gentle rhythm, of motion, is created which brings about relaxation, spontaneity, and tranquility. During the experience, members of the group often sing lullabies or intone and chant words or phrases. Each person takes his place in the "cradle" until everyone has had the experience. The crib technique is an effective way of breaking through a cold, detached group and of escaping the monotony of conventional talk. The kind of tenderness this approach engenders is often radically unlike the early experiences of members of the group. Many individuals—men and women—state that they cannot remember being held, "cradled," or rocked as very young children. Discussions following this approach have often focussed on maternal or paternal rejection and other experiences of rejection, both from the past and in the present. Almost consistently, people emerge from this experience high, alive, feeling wonderful. The motion, the rhythm, the flow, the gentle rocking all contribute to a sense of elation and peace.

### Meditation and Encounter

In this approach, a circle is formed and one person is in the center. The leader makes a brief statement: "We'll begin with two or three minutes of silent meditation. Close your eyes and empty your mind of all thought; just let new feelings and thoughts sail freely through you." In about three minutes the leader continues: "When you are tapped on the shoulder, enter the center of the circle and encounter the person who is there. Meet him or her either verbally or nonverbally; in some way touch the person. Then withdraw from the circle, close your eyes, and tap the person on your right."

Each person in the circle encounters the individual in the center. When the last person completes his encounter, he remains in the center of the circle. The individual who had been in the center takes his place in the circle and the process begins again until everyone in the group has had the experience of being the center of life. In some of my groups this has been an extremely powerful experience. In one that stands out, Mary and Beth were so overwhelmed by the feelings that they burst into tears while in the center. They embraced and, for almost ten minutes, they remained this way, weeping together; no words were spoken; when a sense of fulfillment was experienced, Mary withdrew and returned to the circle. Following this experience, many people have expressed the feeling of being deeply affected by the intimacy, the number of tender embraces, the whispering of gentle, loving words, or just the feeling of being touched. This approach offers an opportunity for solitude, a way to be in communion with a whole group, and a means of person-to-person encounter in the center of the circle. It releases both verbal and nonverbal capacities for dialogue and meditation. I have found that it is most effective in depth and intensity, in spontaneity and freedom of encountering, when a group has been together awhile and has had moments of unity and communion but (although individuals feel comfortable and free) a lull or period of stagnation has developed.

I have used all four procedures in a single group, consecutively, and the group members indicated that it was one of our most valuable meetings together. However, my own feeling is that, if individual and group awareness and sensitivity are evolving naturally, if confrontations and encounters (physical, mental, social, and spiritual) are emerging to create experiences of freedom, spontaneity, meaning, intimacy, and sharing, it is unnecessary (and even interfering) to introduce sensory awareness and other encounter approaches. Further, when such methods are introduced, although individuals should be encouraged to say "yes" to participating in them, an individual who insists on staying out, with his own state of being, should be respected.

In appropriate moments, I have found many other kinds of sensitivity methods useful. In bodily awareness exercises, for example, the individual is asked to be aware of his place in the room, of his presence as a unique individual, of the space that surrounds him; he is asked to be aware of his head, his face, his arms, his stomach, his navel, his legs, to be really aware of each part of his body, to move slowly, attentively, from head to toe, to stay with his own breathing, to move parts of his body and be aware of each movement. These forms of bodily awareness and relatedness are sometimes followed by movements toward other people. The individual is asked to move around the room, to approach every person in the group and shake hands with the person, fully noticing the other's face, looking directly into the person, "eyeball to eyeball"; he may be asked to rub shoulders or backs or buttocks. He may be asked to select one person for special encountering, touching the person's face or other parts of his body, embracing the person or making threatening and aggressive gestures toward the person—pushing or pulling. In each instance he attends to the exchange, to the flow of feeling between the one and the other. He notices; he is aware. The individual may lie on the floor and feel his body touching the surface material. He may become aware of the feel and texture of his clothing or of his skin. Through such approaches, vibrations are aroused within the person and between persons; the individual is in touch with himself, aware of his senses individually and as a unit; and he is in touch with others. He is exercising capacities rarely used and becoming increasingly sensitive to himself and others, aware of his presence and his relationships, and actualizing potentials. A kind of vibrancy, aliveness, and animation develops in which strangers dispense with conventional formalities and introductions and come to see, actually and fully see, each person as an individual self. In the process, within the sharing and the feeling of having participated individually yet in the same world of experience with others, a feeling of being alive as a person and of being in a group emerges and with it a sense of openness and trust.

In the encounter approaches, a number of methods are used to promote intimacy. The members are asked to go around the circle and give first impressions of each person in the group; to close their eyes and depict in their minds images as symbols of each person in the group. They may be asked to select the person most detached from the group, put him in the center, and make direct physical or verbal contact with him. Sometimes each person expresses freely (as he moves around the group) how he feels at the moment; or each person is asked to encounter the person he likes least or is most uncomfortable with or the one he likes most and feels freest with. This may be done with each pair, in turn, entering the center of the circle and non-verbally or verbally carrying out the encounter. Physical threats and gestures may be used as well as hostile or affectionate phrases. The individuals may be paired off and given five or ten minutes to come to know one another. They are told to ask direct, personal questions, to get right into the heart of the relationship as quickly as possible. Every ten minutes the partners change until each person has met every other.

One person may be asked to relate a current problem that represents a pervasive threat in his life; the task of the other members of the group is to listen carefully and to make remarks or ask questions that will facilitate the individual's exploring and searching. Listening and enabling the creating person is the function of the audience; open, direct, honest exploring is the task of the troubled individual. The group may be structured so that each person is asked to concentrate on the most destructive interpersonal act he has inflicted on another person or had inflicted on him by another. The group struggles with this silently, perhaps for five or ten minutes, and then each person is asked to share the experience with the group. Or the members are asked to focus on the happiest moment, the peak moment, or the most beautiful act expressed toward or by another, and, following a time of silent exploration, these are shared with the group.

Many other ways are being developed to foster trust, openness, intimacy, awareness, individuality, communion, and human meaning in groups. As I see it, these techniques have value as catalysts in developing interpersonal meaning. The specific approach used in a group depends upon the individuals involved, the time available, the nature and purpose of their coming together, and their associations in the everyday world.

Each, in its own way, offers possibilities for release of tensions, removal of conventional barriers and defenses, awakening to new sensory experience, to new meaning and direction and the development of value in group life. Each leader of a group discovers his own methods of actualization of human potentials toward increasing individuality and encounter. As for me, I find immediate significance in the sensitivity techniques as ways of evoking real life and breaking through monotony and deadness in a group. I see the value of using these methods spontaneously where they fit a particular group, rather than automatically applying them. Though such techniques may give an immediate feeling of trust, openness, awareness, or nearness to oneself and others, full development of these feelings requires a more intense, longer range struggle within oneself and with others. Such approaches lead into deeper regions of self-awareness and deeper levels of dialogue with others where there is continuity and follow-through in the group. Obviously, there is a difference between the brief, short-term encounters in interpersonal relations and the longitudinal meetings—a difference in depth, intimacy, fullness, and value.

### The Flower Turn-On[1]

I wish now to concentrate, in more detail, on an encounter method that has involved many significant dimensions of myself, that has enabled me to clarify and resolve unfinished matters and to reach new levels of self-awareness.

When "The Flower Turn-On" has been right in timing and structuring for a particular group, it has been an extremely vital procedure, but it has not always been effective with groups in facilitating human values when

---

[1] I was introduced to this approach by Ben Finney of San Jose State College, but my application of it is a reflection of my own being in a group and the improvisation that comes from meeting the immediate conditions of unique life with others.

used too early, in the wrong way, or with the wrong group.

Rather than talking about the method, I will relate my own experience with it in one specific group, a group of gifted adolescents enrolled in a special residential summer program. During the regular academic year they attended highly conventional public schools that offered almost no opportunity for creative expression. The group contained Negro youngsters from a junior high school and Caucasian youngsters from a senior high school. They were selected for the summer project by teacher recommendations, interviews, and test data on creative abilities.

In making arrangements to participate in the program, I had suggested that I come, explore the setting, and find my own place and group. In the school, from a number of offerings, each person selected his own sequence of activities; the 100 adolescents had arranged themselves in eight groups. After several hours of wandering from group to group, I became discouraged; I began to feel that I was an outsider, estranged from the whole situation and lonely. There was no invitation to join any of the groups, and I was not motivated to try to push my way in. None of the activities seemed real to me; there was much talking but little genuine involvement. I noticed, too, that the Negro and white youths were almost totally segregated. Since there was freedom in the school for individuals to choose their own groups, I concluded that the choice was influenced primarily by race rather than interest or talent. In this state of estrangement, I asked the director to call an assembly of all the students. Somehow, I wanted to meet these youngsters, to come to know them, and I wanted them to meet me.

In the assembly, I expressed my immediate feelings of isolation and loneliness. It was clear from the response of the youngsters that many of them were also feeling removed from real life, cut off from genuine involvement, and lonely. It was the beginning of a vital group process. At the end of the meeting I asked those who wished to continue in a self-awareness group to remain behind. Twenty people stayed—fifteen adolescents and five faculty members, including myself. Seven of the youngsters were Negroes and eight where white. I suggested that one way of developing self-awareness and coming alive as a group was through a method called "The Flower Turn-On." Rather than explaining what it was, I suggested that we try it together.

In this procedure, each person selects a live flower, one that he feels he can relate to, one that he likes or dislikes, one that reminds him of himself or is very different, one that recalls someone he loves or he rejects.

Since there were no fields or gardens in the area, I suggested that we go to a florist shop, where each person could select his flower. This turned out to be a really important part of the whole experience—going into town as a group, the feeling of being together, the growing excitement of entering the shop. To my amazement some of these youngsters had never been in a florist shop, had never purchased a flower or had one given to them as a gift. All of these factors combined to create a buoyancy and gaiety among us as we entered the store. The shopkeeper immediately felt the excitement and meaning in the activity and not only stayed in the background but encouraged us to take our time in deciding and even invited us to explore the back room to get the full range of alternatives. Each flower was selected with care; the moment it was selected the youngsters withdrew into the background to a private place. The alive expressions were infectious when the "right" flower was discovered. Marion especially intrigued me. She was a tall, heavy person with a squeezed-in body and rounded shoulders. She chose a straight, firm, tall mum with a large white blossom; it created an electric spark in her. She jumped with joy and her face was absolutely radiant. Gently she lifted the flower from the vase and held it close. She was in a trance and her entire body seemed to expand and relax; her stooped, squeezed-in shoulders straightened and she stood tall, receptive, and beautiful—like the mum she had chosen. "You mean this is mine to keep?" she asked, unbelieving. "Even when this is over I can keep it?" When I nodded affirmatively, she exclaimed with joy, "Oh, I've never had a flower of my own before. I've never had a flower given to me!" Variations of this excitement, this elation, occurred with each youngster. Nearly an hour later we left the shop. In the process of flower selection we had developed a feeling of community, a very special feeling, and we were important to one another. I invited the group to join me in the living room of the apartment in which I was staying; some of us sat on the sofa and some on the floor.

"The Flower Turn-On" begins with a 20- to 30-minute musical selection, preferably classical music or music with a major theme that includes minor variations and reaches peak moments and crescendos. Some of the most facilitating pieces I have used are David Oistrakh's playing of Beethoven's *Violin Concerto* (2nd movement), Beethoven's *Symphony No. 6, The Pastoral Symphony* (1st movement), and Vivaldi's *The Four Seasons*. However, for the adolescent group, since none of these records was available, I used the second side of the music from *Dr. Zhivago,* and it turned out to be a good choice. I gave the following directions:

"We'll begin this experience listening to music from *Dr. Zhivago.* During the recording, it is important to maintain absolute silence. Let yourself enter into a relationship with your flower. Come to know it as a whole and in its details. Open yourself to the color, the fragrance, the touch and feel of it. Notice its texture and shape, the patterns it forms. See it as it is, really relate to it—let your own feelings go with it. If it arouses feelings of sadness or joy, go into these feelings—let them flow. If it brings happiness or suffering, be these feel-

ings—enter them completely. The music and the flower
may remind you of your relationships with important
people in your life, of your own desires and dreams and
fears, of your own self. You may recall occasions of
mourning or death or moments of very special happiness
and love. Follow these paths, immerse yourself in them
—let life take root in you. When the recording is over,
each of us will share his experience."

Following the music, I extended an open invitation to
begin the sharing. Several people were crying and the
expressions on their faces told me that they wished to
remain silent. I noticed that two of the youngsters,
Lorna and Bob, had moved closer together. They were
sitting on the floor and were communicating with their
flowers—a kind of silent dialogue between them, coupled
with touching and caressing their flowers. They radiated
happiness. I looked in their direction, but neither
wished to speak. I waited several more minutes and
then decided to share my own experience. I have found
that, if no one else is ready and if I myself have something really vital to share, revealing myself encourages
others to be open and trusting.

"My flower (I had selected a yellow daisy) reminds
me of the gold in my children's hair. It brings back
memories of special joy, and my reminiscing is a good
feeling. Inside just now I feel relaxed and happy to be
here. The music and each petal of my flower has its
place. Together in them I feel a unity. Each of us is
like the petals of this flower—vibrant with life; together
we are whole. I see the center of my daisy as the center
of existence; the center of me is the being I am. I see
myself running through fields of daisies—thousands,
millions of daisies blowing freely in the wind. Sunshine
radiates everywhere, and all at once I am filled with
ecstasy, with a desire to love everyone. Everything becomes bright and beautiful. I want to share this joy, this
passion for life. (Pause) Yet, underneath, painful feelings tug at me. I see the beauty of my flower, and yet

its perfection, its exquisite individuality saddens me, for all at once I know that it is dying. I become aware of suffering in the world, of young people, children, and families dying, being killed. I think of the burning and destruction and death in Vietnam and the violence and riots and deaths in our homes and in our streets. I think of poverty and degradation, of life in its most diminished forms. I am overcome with the terribleness of man's inhumanity to man. Why—why must it be? There is no answer, but inside just now, at this moment, there is agony in being alive, agony, too, in being happy, being in love in the midst of fragmentation, insensitivity, insanity, death. I am struggling with these feelings, the living and the dying parts of me and the living and the dying parts of my flower."

Wilma spoke next: "My flower, this little yellow rose, is like me—just a bud, closed, with maybe a promise that someday it will blossom. I have this feeling of being little, of being afraid; I want to open myself and let people see me as I am inside. But I'm afraid that if people know who I really am, they'll reject me, and it's hard, oh so hard, just to be yourself. If you show the small, surface side, you'll be accepted. But the inside of me is like this rose—tough, firm, and hardy—and the outside is delicate, fragile, and tender. So I show the outside and people treat me like a child, small and immature. I arouse their sympathy and get what I want out of pity. But I'm not satisfied. I wish I had the courage just to be me, to let people know my strength and my weakness, to let people see me as I am."

Donna, who had been crying throughout the experience, was struggling to speak: "I hope I can get through this because I'm not really sad—I'm happy—happier than I have been in a long time. I had decided to make up a story to impress you all (she stopped, cried very hard for several minutes) . . . and . . . uh . . . I want to tell the truth. I'm always saying the right things to make people like me, and sometimes it's so lonely being liked. But here I feel I can be myself. I don't have any big secret to tell. I'm just happy. When the music was playing, I wanted to dance. I had to control myself because the muscles in my body moved with the music. I'm just happy and I don't know why. But I'm glad I'm here."

Bob related his experience: "I'm happy too. I've been wanting to ask Lorna for a date from the first day of school. But I didn't have the courage. I was afraid she'd reject me. While *Dr. Zhivago* was playing, I started talking to Lorna (Lorna moved closer to Bob) with my rose." (Lorna and Bob exchanged flowers, embraced with the flowers, and moved them freely into dancing motions.)

Each person shared his private experience with his flower, and in the process a whole range of interactions opened. From the individual explorations came dialogues between the youngsters and between the faculty and the youngsters. Person-to-person feedback paved the way to new awareness. At the end there was a discussion of the summer program and why genuine life was not evolving in the school. Through "The Flower Turn-On" we developed a deeper feeling as a group; we were persons together, integrated as human beings. One of the faculty members said that it was the first time during the summer that she really felt related to the teen-agers, that she really felt she could be herself, that she really felt the value of being in a group. Some of the dialogues involved struggles with indifference, prejudice, and rejection; others involved facing fears of being a Negro in a Caucasian group and vice versa. These fears, when shared, no longer caused distortion and detachment. In the process, the separating elements were joined; teen-agers and faculty walked away together, feeling warm and intimate, with arms around one another, singing songs of joy and happiness.

## Concluding Comments

From my experiences in groups—the meaningful development of spontaneous, intimate human relations, and the numerous peak moments in dialogue, in confrontation, in sensory awareness, in body expression, in sensitive awakenings—I have struggled to understand and to know the nature of individual life, the nature of person-to-person encounter, and the nature of unity and communion. I do not believe that any set of prinicples, or techniques, or theories, or concepts can characterize, can capture the ongoing moment-by-moment life of a group. Ideas, techniques, principles, when spontaneously applied to the unique situation, can sometimes facilitate development of trust, openness, spontaneity, and love among human beings; but these values have their own particular forms of expression in different groups, and the specific individuals involved must determine their own way of life. The challenge of each group is to discover the way, through struggle with distortions, barriers, and defenses; to create an authentic, living process via self-exploration and self-awareness, through feedback that is not evaluative but seeks only to clarify and open, through peak moments of intimacy and communion, through sharing of the vital within oneself and in one's relations, sharing that is not mere reporting and repeating but that, in itself, is a form of actualizing potentials.

I see, consistently, two significant values operating: being an individual, purely, honestly, and fully, centering in one's own thoughts, feelings, preferences, and interests; and being within a community of human beings, or within a single relationship, which means, at times, steeping oneself in the world of the other, transcending the private, individual needs and desires, sacrificing one's own self-centered truths by becoming unified and connected with other human beings. Often the individual can pursue his own development, his own perceptions of an essential truth in himself or in others without in any way denying or impeding the growth of the group as a whole. This, then, is the crucial value—self-discovery and self-awareness, insisting on being oneself, purely and completely, moment by moment. Often the group can experience unity and communion without, in any way, requiring personal sacrifice or personal denial or the leaping away from oneself into the world of others, away from one's own private interests or goals. When there is a genuine conflict of values between the individual and the group as a whole, or even between persons, something has to give, or only tugging and pulling remain, and the impact of irresolvable forces. There are times when individuality looks more like selfishness, egoism, and narcissism, more like a concern for oneself, first and always. Sometimes the group can give way and take the path of one person, alter its course and search for an integration that recognizes and includes each person authentically. Sometimes the individual can give way, stop hanging on to himself as the main or only value in life, and realize that being part of a group, part of a community, is also an essential human requirement. Individual life, person-to-person life, and group life—each has an essential meaning. Being extremely, consistently, and determinedly in one of these paths to the exclusion of the others or at the expense of the others represents a limited and warped orientation. A philosophy of extreme individualism comes close to hedonism and narcissism. A way of life based on the single relationship comes close to narrowness, rigidity, and exclusiveness. A philosophy of group existence comes close to submission, adjustment, and conformity. The ideal, healthy way of life, as I see it, involves a balance of these experiences, an involvement, concern, and actualization of each to some degree. At times, I sacrifice or abandon my own personal interests to join my wife or child or friend in some mutual activity or experience because, in that moment, the relationship is strengthened and enriched by self-denial. At other times, I stand by my individual interest, even when it threatens a relationship, because my own development in that moment is crucial. Each represents an important human value; I must choose, when there is a conflict of interests, to pursue the one course or the other. From my experiences in solitude, in single relationships, in groups, I have concluded that the person who constantly chooses one of these ways of living and excludes the others is a restricted person; while actualizing one capacity, other vital human values are thwarted and denied. The fully integrated person does not always pursue his private ends or the benefits of a single relationship or the values of communal life. There are times in a relationship when I am the center, when my world is the main attraction for both of us, and vice versa. At other times, you and I pursue our individual paths, without limiting or denying. But a genuine life involves shifting from the one to the other, involves give and take, which requires self-abandonment, self-transcendence, and even compromise—not compromise that is reducing but compromise that has a meaning, though perhaps not quite the excitement, flavor, and intensity of one's own pure, private ecstasy. There are times when the individual and the group are legitimately in conflict. If each person went his separate way, something of value would be lost. Without some degree of altruism, without self-transcendence, there can be no permanent relationship, no permanent family or group ties. I believe that each of these structures is an essential human value and that full self-actualization means experiencing and valuing them.

When there is a realization of individuality, of relationship, of communal living, human horizons are enriched, expanded, deepened, and sensitized. We can learn from others not only the meaning of uniqueness and individuality, not only the meaning of group life, but also the meaning of self-abandonment and self-sacrifice and the valid moments of group abandonment and group sacrifice. In other words, when a critical situation is at stake, sometimes the single individual is more important than the group, but the reverse is also true. If the issue can be settled through confrontation, clarification, feedback, and new awareness, where neither the person nor the group is denied, this is the ideal solution. But when there is no authentic way to reach unity, then a bridge must be formed that joins the one force with the other. Withdrawal, indifference, rejection, egocentrism only create bigger cleavages and gaps. Bonds and ties in human life are essential to man's fulfillment, as are individuality and solitude; in the crisis, the bridge to relatedness is created through intimacy and love. Something in the way of individual or group value is lost, but something vital and essential to human existence is gained.

## REFERENCES

Gibran, Kahlil. *Sand and Foam.* New York: Alfred A. Knopf, 1926.

Rilke, Rainer Maria. *Letters To a Young Poet.* Tr. by M. D. Herter Norton. New York: W. W. Norton, 1954.

Schutz, William C. *Joy. Expanding Human Awareness.* New York: Grove Press, Inc., 1967.

CHAPTER 5

# *Heuristic*

# Research

The impetus for writing this chapter came from several sources: my own growing dissatisfaction with conventional research as a means to study significant problems, issues, and processes with reference to man and human experience; the questions of my students and colleagues; and my wish to clarify with others my own research philosophy and perspective.

Rather than listing a series of research concepts and abstractions, which would be a fragmented and mechanical effort and which I would approach unenthusiastically, I have decided to explore an actual research experience, which distinguishes the discovery process from that of verification and corroboration. In this presentation, I shall outline the significant dimensions of what I am calling *heuristic research,* that is, a research approach that encourages an individual to discover and methods that enable him to investigate further by himself.

Because of its recent significance and its impact on my own awareness and way of life, I have chosen my study of loneliness (1961) to express and illustrate the nature and meaning of heuristic research.

[1] Reprinted, with revisions, from "Heuristic Research" by Clark Moustakas in *Challenges of Humanistic Psychology,* James F. T. Bugental (Ed.). New York: McGraw-Hill Book Co., 1967, by permission of the publishers.

*Sources of the Study*

My study of loneliness had no design or purpose, no object or end, and no hypotheses or assumptions. While I was faced with a question or problem (whether or not to agree to major heart surgery that might restore my daughter to health or result in her death) in the beginning, I was not inquiring into the nature or meaning of loneliness and its impact on the individual in modern society. However, the urgency for making this critical decision plunged me into the experience of feeling utterly alone and cut off from human companionship. The entire process of facing the terror and consequences of major heart surgery or an uncertain future and a premature death initiated my search into loneliness. At first, the search was a search into my own self, looking deeply within, trying to discover and be aware, trying to find the right way to proceed, and experiencing a sense of isolation when each path or journey ended with a question mark.

Experiences of lonely self-reflection came at unexpected moments, in the midst of a crowd of people, in response to a word or phrase in conversation. Many different kinds of situations evoked an inner process of doubt, uncertainty, and isolation. Sometimes I awakened in the night, and being overwhelmed by images and feelings and thoughts, I tried to draw from deep down within myself a single answer, a single direction, which would utilize in an integrated form all the data—my experiences with my daughter, talks with physicians, and published reports on heart surgery. The initial journey was an attempt to discover the one true way to proceed; it involved a process of self-inquiry, which was not planned but simply happened, which was not carefully sampled but occurred spontaneously at unexpected times and places. While no answer came to the problem of surgery, I became aware that at the center of my world was a deep and pervasive feeling of loneliness.

With this feeling came the tentative realization that loneliness is a capacity or source in man for new searching, awareness, and inspiration—that when the outside world ceases to have a meaning, when support and confirmation are lacking or are not adequate to assuage human suffering, when doubt and uncertainty overwhelm a person, then the individual may contemplate life from the depths of his own self and in nature. For me, this was a discovery that in a crucial and compelling crisis, in spite of comfort and sympathy from others, one can feel utterly and completely alone, that, at bottom, the experience of loneliness exists in its own right as a source of power and creativity, as a source of insight and direction, as a requirement of living no matter how much love and affirmation one receives in his work and in his relationships with others.

Thus, the beginning steps of my research into loneliness (which at the time I did not know I was researching) involved not a question of the nature of loneliness, not a question of its restorative, creative, or destructive impact on the individual, but a struggle and search into another problem. Much later I realized that loneliness is often experienced by men who must make crucial decisions that will have major consequences in the lives of other men. Through inner exploration and study, I sought to find a solution that would integrate the facts into one clear pattern. The significance of inner searching for deeper awareness as a relevant step in research is cogently expressed by Polanyi in his book *Science, Faith and Society*:

> *Scientific knowing consists in discerning Gestalten that are aspects of reality.* I have here called this "intuition"; in later writings I have described it as a tacit co-efficient of a scientific theory, by which it bears on experience as a token of reality. Thus it foresees yet indeterminate manifestations of the experience on which it bears.
>
> Every interpretation of nature, whether scientific, non-scientific or anti-scientific, is based on some intuitive

conception of the general nature of things. . . . But in spite of much beautiful work . . . we still have no clear conception of how discovery comes about. The main difficulty has been pointed out by Plato in the *Meno*. He says that to search for the solution of a problem is an absurdity. For either you know what you are looking for, and then there is no problem; or you do not know what you are looking for, and then you are not looking for anything and cannot expect to find anything. . . . A potential discovery may be thought to attract the mind which will reveal it—inflaming the scientist with creative desire and imparting to him intimations that guide him from clue to clue and from surmise to surmise. The testing hand, the straining eye, the ransacked brain, may all be thought to be labouring under the common spell of a potential discovery striving to emerge into actuality.

Experiences in meditation and self-searching, in intuitive and mystical reachings, and in hours and hours of silent midnight walking paved the way to a formulation of my study of loneliness, a formulation that emerged clearly during my observations of hospitalized children. In the hospital I began to see how lonely feelings impelled young children to seek a compassionate voice and a warm, friendly face; I began to see how young children separated from their parents could often be more completely involved in the struggle with loneliness than in the painful experiences connected with illness and surgery; I began to see how children separated from their parents underwent a period of protest and resistance against separation, against the mechanical actions and fixed faces and gestures of the hospital combine. I also observed a gradual deterioration of protest, rebellion, and self-assertion and, in their place, a deep sense of isolation, lonely weeping, withdrawal, depression, and numbness. In general, I witnessed a basic, pervasive feeling of dehumanization, which sought to repress lonely feelings and the whole range of human emotions that characterize the alive and growing child.

## THE TOTAL PERSON AS A RESEARCH METHOD

When I saw that these dimensions of loneliness were almost totally ignored, misunderstood, and misinterpreted by hospital aides, nurses, and doctors, I decided, using the hospital situation and my own intuitive awareness as a beginning, to try to understand loneliness, how it fitted into the perceptions and behavior of hospitalized children, and the way in which it existed in myself and others. I decided to listen to the experiences of children in the hospital with objectivity and warmth, not taking notes and making records and thus objectifying, but keeping the focus of my interest on the experience of loneliness itself, on the essence of the experience through the person's rendering of it and relating of it. Objectivity, in this connection, means seeing what an experience *is* for another person, not what causes it, not why it exists, not how it can be defined and classified. It means seeing attitudes, beliefs, and feelings of the person as they exist for him at the moment he is experiencing them, perceiving them whole, as a unity. I set out to know the meaning of loneliness, not by defining and categorizing, but by experiencing it directly and through the lives of others, as a simple reality of life in the way that Moore describes reality in *Principia Ethica*:

> My point is that "good" is a simple notion, just as "yellow" is a simple notion; that, just as you cannot, by any manner of means, explain to any one who does not already know it, what yellow is, so you cannot explain what good is. Definitions of the kind that I was asking for, definitions which describe the real nature of the object or notion denoted by a word, and which do not merely tell us what the word is used to mean, are only possible when the object or notion in question is something complex. You can give a definition of a horse, because a horse has many different properties and qualities, all of which you can enumerate. But when you have enumerated them all, when you have reduced a horse to

his simplest terms, then you can no longer define those terms. They are simply something which you think of or perceive, and to any one who cannot think of or perceive them, you can never, by any definition, make their nature known.

Thus I set out to discover the meaning of loneliness in its simplest terms, desiring to perceive the experience of being lonely in its absolutely native state. At the same time, I knew from my own experiences and from my conversations with hospitalized children that loneliness itself could not be communicated by words or defined in its essence, that loneliness could not be known except by persons who are open to their own senses and aware of their own experiences. I set out to discover the nature of lonely experience by intimate encounter with other persons. A quotation from Polanyi's *Personal Knowledge* may clarify this point:

> To say that the discovery of objective truth in science consists in the apprehension of a rationality which commands our respect and arouses our contemplative admiration; that such discovery, while using the experience of our senses as clues, transcends this experience by embracing the vision of a reality beyond the impression of our senses, a vision which speaks for itself in guiding us to an ever deeper understanding of reality—such an account of scientific procedure would be generally shrugged aside as out-dated Platonism: a piece of mystery-mongering unworthy of an enlightened age. Yet it is precisely on this conception of objectivity that I wish to insist. . . . Into every act of knowing there enters a passionate contribution of the person knowing what is known, and . . . this coefficient is no mere imperfection but a vital component of his knowledge.

## Entering into the Experience

My way of studying loneliness, in its essential form, was to put myself into an open, ready state, into the lonely experiences of hospitalized children, and to let these experiences become the focus of my world. I listened. I watched. I stood by. In dialogue with the child, I tried to put into words the deep regions of his experience. Sometimes my words touched the child in the interior of his feelings, and he began to weep; sometimes the child formed words in response to my presence, and thus he began to break through his numbness and the dehumanizing impact of the hospital atmosphere and practice. At this point, loneliness became my existence. It entered into every facet of my world—into my teaching, my interviews in therapy, my conversations with friends, my home life. Without reference to time or place or structure, somehow (more intentionally than accidentally) the theme came up. I was clearly aware that, exhaustively and fully, and in careful manner, I was searching for, studying, and inquiring into the nature and impact of loneliness. I was totally involved and immersed in this search for a pattern and meaning that would reveal the various dimensions of loneliness in modern life. This was research in the sense of a close searching and inquiring into the nature of a reality of human experience. I was certainly not studying loneliness simply as an intellectual or academic question, in a detached manner, but rather in an integrative, living form; becoming part of the lonely experiences of others; being within lonely moments in living; being involved, committed, interested, concerned, while at the same time aware of an emerging pattern and relatedness. Facts, knowledge, insights were accumulating as I listened and later recorded and studied; but, at the same time, there were intuitive visions, feelings, sensings that went beyond anything I could record or think about or know in a factual sense. At the center of the lonely existence were ineffable, indescribable feelings and experiences, a presence which I felt in a unified and essential way. I had gone "wide open," at moments ceasing to be a separate individual, but wholly related to the other person, leaving something behind of my own intuitive vision, and comprehension while, at the same time, taking something away—very much in the manner that Steinbeck and Ricketts approached their study of the *Sea of Cortez*:

> Let's see what we see, record what we find, and not fool ourselves with conventional scientific strictures— in that lonely and uninhabited Gulf our boat and ourselves would change it the moment we entered. By going there, we would bring a new factor to the Gulf. Let us consider that factor and not be betrayed by this myth of permanent objective reality. If it exists at all it is only available in pickled tatters or in distorted flashes. "Let us go," we said, "into the Sea of Cortez, realizing that we become forever a part of it; that our rubber boots slogging through a flat of eelgrass, that the rocks we turn over in a tide pool, make us truly and permanently a factor in the ecology of the region. We shall take something away from it, but we shall leave something too." And if we seem a small factor in a huge pattern, nevertheless it is of relative importance. We take a tiny colony of soft corals from a rock in a little water world. And that isn't terribly important to the tide pool. Fifty miles away the Japanese shrimp boats are dredging with overlapping scoops, bringing up tons of shrimps, rapidly destroying the ecological balance of the whole region. That isn't very important in the world. And six thousand miles away the great bombs are falling on London and the stars are not moved thereby. None of it is important or all of it is.

Thus I entered into a formal study of loneliness, taking into it my own growing awareness, the discovery of myself as a lonely person, my experiences in the hospital, and my many moments, conversations, dialogues, and discussions with other persons—children in school settings, who spoke freely and openly and wrote themes expressing their lonely experiences; parents and young adults in therapy, who struggled and found it painful to speak of loneliness but who, once initiated in this journey, were able to recapture and create in a living sense moments of the past and current feelings of isolation and solitude; and friends and colleagues, who could reveal the intimate depth of lonely experiences. I steeped myself in a world of loneliness, letting my life take root and unfold in it, letting its dimensions and meanings and forms evolve in its own timetable and dynamics.

## The Use of the Literature

The study was culminated in my readings of published reports on loneliness and lonely experiences. But this was a point near the end, not at the beginning, where it might have acted to predispose and predetermine and color my own growing awareness. I began to study volumes of biography and autobiography of individuals who dramatically exemplified lonely lives. Among other persons, those who captured my interest were Emily Dickinson, Abraham Lincoln, Woodrow Wilson, Benedict Arnold, and Ned Langford. I also followed the lonely experiences of Herman Buhl in his journey to the highest peak of the Himalayas, Admiral Byrd alone on an advanced base in Antarctica, Saint-Exupéry lost in the desert, and other persons involved in extreme situations of isolation. I studied the autobiographical volumes of Hiss and Chambers, as well as many political analyses of their confrontation and its implications, including the numerous volumes of the House Un-American Activities Committee and the ten volumes of the trial transcript, to see more fully the lonely consequences of infamy and mass public rejection. I discovered additional nuances of the meaning of loneliness from the studies of Frieda Fromm-Reichmann of the loneliness of mental patients, Margaret Wood's *Paths of Loneliness,* Eithne Tabor's *Songs of a Psychotic,* Karl Menninger's *Love against Hate,* David Riesman's *The Lonely Crowd,* Erich Fromm's *Escape from Freedom,* Thomas Wolfe's *Hills Beyond,* Sullivan's *Interpersonal Theory of Psychiatry,* and the numerous articles and reports appearing in newspapers and journals, accounts that could be understood both as attempts to escape and overcome loneliness and as evolutions of deeper sensitivity and awareness that enabled unique and creative expressions of loneliness in poetry, music, literature, and other art forms.

When a pattern began to emerge with reference to the nature and function of loneliness in individual experience and in modern living, the formal study came to an end. At this point the framework and detail, the clarification of loneliness, had been formed; it was possible to differentiate and refine its meaning, to expand and illustrate its nature and relevance in human experience. Thus what started as a hospital study of loneliness became an extended research into the phenomenon of loneliness. The conditions and factors that initiated and characterized the study were as follows: (1) a crisis, which created a question or problem; (2) a search of self in solitude, from which emerged a recognition of the significance of loneliness both as a creative urging and as a frightening and disturbing experience; (3) an expanding awareness through being open to lonely life and lonely experiences, through watching, listening, and feeling, and through conversation, dialogue, and discussion; (4) a steeping of myself in the deeper regions of loneliness, so that it became the ingredient of my being, the center of my world; (5) an intuitive grasping of the patterns of loneliness, of related aspects and different associations, until an integrated vision and awareness emerged; (6) further clarification, delineation, and refinement through studies of lonely lives, lonely experiences, and published reports on loneliness; and (7) creation of a form, a manuscript, in which to project and express the various forms, themes, and values of loneliness and in which to present its creative powers, as well as the anxiety it arouses in discontent, restlessness, and boredom, and the strategies used in attempting to overcome and escape loneliness.

## HUMAN VALIDATION

Since the publication of *Loneliness,* I have received approximately five hundred letters that verify and validate my portrayal of loneliness in modern life—its nature, its beauty, and its terror. My correspondents confirmed the meaning and essence of loneliness that had emerged from my research; each of these persons portrayed the uniqueness of lonely experience and its powers in drawing upon untouched capacities and resources, in evolving new creations, and in expanding awareness, sensitivity, and compassion, as well as the extreme pain, grief, despair, and impotency that often accompany the urge to discover, to answer the challenges and problems of living, to face genuinely and authentically separation, illness, and death. I have selected five letters as illustrations of response and confirmation:

1. Today I read your book, *Loneliness.* It was one of those rare experiences that seem to come "just in time." Somehow I wanted you to know that I appreciated your sharing with me the "feelings and insights" expressed in this book—for you see it is not just a book but a kind of communication not often experienced.

The greatest value I received from sharing this communication was that when circumstances of life seem to be taking from us our right to be then we must re-affirm our faith in our own being and refuse to be pushed aimlessly along. Thank you for giving some impetus to this re-affirmation.

2 Having just completed your book *Loneliness,* I must thank you for such an articulate and sensitive presentation of basic truths relating to human suffering. Since the sudden and premature death of my husband in September, 1959, and the agonizing period following it when, primarily motivated by the two babies I had been left to rear alone, I struggled to retain sanity, I have had a deep interest in loneliness, its causes, its effects. Your book clarified a number of matters for me.

3 I read your beautifully written book of *Loneliness* and was very impressed with its truthfulness. I do be-

lieve, however, that the subject matter has been expounded many times by many writers and authors, but because of the lack of a formal education I never realized that anyone could possible see me in these dimensions. I think I know the meaning of this subject as well as, if not better, than most. I need no formal education for this. I have lived, associated myself with, become drawn toward the lonely, and know readily those who are. P.S. I am a janitor. I also work in a print shop. Please forgive the informality.

4    I read those parts which I felt a need to read from *Loneliness* during Christmas vacation. I was deeply affected by the experiences I was able to share. I picked the book up again and read and was surprised at the wonderment of being able to experience as though never before these same journeys through loneliness.

I felt that my very feelings were caught up and understood by the author—that a friendly someone could write what I had felt, but hadn't been able to express in words.

I gained something from this reading, partly that I don't have to feel that being lonely is wasteful—that I don't have to be busy every minute, to be a complete person. Before I was afraid to be lonely, afraid I was just wasting precious time and afraid that I wasn't adequate enough within myself.

For someone who usually rambles endlessly on when affected by something I can't really think of anything else to say, perhaps later, right now I'm still experiencing it.

5    Not long ago I talked to a group of people with considerable feeling in my presentation, pointing their attention to the need to be individual and independent centers for living, each man in his own. I had been able to suggest that this was an avenue also to deepest companionship and significant social value. After my lecture, I noticed that the group disbanded quickly and individuals went off by themselves, not even coming up to me as they usually do. My first impulse was to feel that my lecture had fallen flat. Later I learned that the opposite was the case with several of the group, at least. People are hungry to be their own authorities in basic life matters and, spurred by my own expression in these matters, they wanted it all the more, meaning they had to leave me to my own, too.

I need not tell you that I think you are doing just the

right thing in forming your experience as you are doing. The vacuum of "being," if not filled with the substance of life-realized in depth (as you are doing), will gain so much power that our people will collapse inwardly in the clutter of their own psychic debris.

The loneliness each man feels is his hunger for life itself, not only life in his being, but life in the being of creation, past, present and future. Your book allows the reader to recognize his own vacuum which is the first step to appreciation of its filling. Had you left your own vacuum uncomposed in expression, you would have left others with nothing (a disparate emptiness); composing it, you gave others not only a chance of recognizing their own, but also a way of composing a view of one's emptiness as one visualizes the cup in a ring, inviting the placement of the pearl of great price. It is the yearning that makes fulfillment possible in the most elemental ranges. It is death present within life, without which there could not be life.

## CONCLUSION

While the subject of the research was loneliness, I have tried to portray the research process itself from its initial steps to its final phases. I now believe in such a process of searching and studying, of being open to significant dimensions of experience in which comprehension and compassion mingle; in which intellect, emotion, and spirit are integrated; in which intuition, spontaneity, and self-exploration are seen as components of unified experience; in which both discovery and creation are reflections of creative research into human ventures, human processes, and human experiences. In conclusion, I quote several passages, which I believe are relevant to this study of heuristic research. Some of the effects of such an approach (selected from an essay by Rogers) are as follows:

In the first place it would tend to do away with the fear of creative subjective speculation. As I talk with graduate students in the behavioral sciences this fear is a very deep one. It cuts them off from any significant discovery. They would be shocked by the writings of a Kepler in his mystical and fanciful searching for likenesses and patterns in nature. They do not recognize that it is out of such fanciful thinking that true science emerges. . . .

A second effect would be to place a stress on disciplined commitment, disciplined *personal* commitment, not methodology. It would be a very healthy emphasis in the behavioral sciences if we could recognize that it is the dedicated, personal search of a disciplined, open-minded individual which discovers and creates new knowledge. No refinement of laboratory or statistical method can do this. . . .

Another effect would be that it would permit a free rein to phenomenological thinking in behavioral science, our effort to understand man and perhaps even the animals from the inside. It would recognize that no type of hypothesis has any special virtue in science save only in its relationship to a meaningful pattern which exists in the universe. . . .

Another and more general effect would be that if the picture of science I have tried to suggest gains some general acceptance in our field then it would give a new dignity to the science of man and to the scientist who commits himself to that field. It would keep the scientist as a human being in the picture at all times, and we would recognize that science is but the lengthened shadow of dedicated human beings.

## REFERENCES

Moore, George E. *Principia Ethica.* New York: Cambridge University Press, 1903. Paperback edition, 1959.

Moustakas, Clark. *Loneliness.* Englewood Cliffs, N.J.: Prentice-Hall, 1961.

Polanyi, Michael. *Personal Knowledge.* Chicago: University of Chicago Press, 1958.

Polanyi, Michael. *Science, Faith and Society.* (First Phoenix ed.) Chicago: University of Chicago Press, 1964.

Rogers, Carl R. Some Thoughts Regarding the Current Philosophy of the Behavioral Sciences. Unpublished paper, Western Behavioral Sciences Institute, La Jolla, Calif., 1964.

Steinbeck, John, & Ricketts, Edward F. *Sea of Cortez.* New York: Viking Press, 1941.

*Individuality and Encounter* searches into the nature of intimate human relationships, the meaning of peak moments in loneliness, in dialogue, in confrontation, in sensory awareness and body expression and in sudden sensitive awakenings. The book explores individual life, the person-to-person encounter and the development of unity and communion in groups. Ideas, principles, feelings, methods are spontaneously expressed in a variety of human situations. Experiences are created in which trust, openness, spontaneity, and love are developed.

To be in touch with oneself means that the individual must be a self and to be a self means that the person perceives and knows life from his own experience; he is rooted in his own existence and he discovers reality and meaning from the knowledge of his own senses. To learn and grow authentically the individual must be a self in these ways: first, open to himself and open to the world; second, free to choose and select from the vantage point of his own capacities, talents and resources, in terms of the person he is; third, free enough and courageous enough to confirm the fitting and deny the non-fitting; in other words to say "yes" to some of life's possibilities and ventures and "no" to others; fourth, he must be responsible for his own choices and actions, learning from mistakes, not being fixed by them or distorted by them but recognizing and accepting them as steps to forward movement and progress and learning too from right choices which confirm decision and action and contribute to growth in attitudes and values. Only by being free to choose and to accept the joys and consequences of decisions does the individual develop values which enable him to establish roots and an identity.

An essential stream of experience in the development of individuality is man's relationship to himself, his capacity to enter into moments of loneliness and solitude and to create from these moments new awareness, feeling, and direction.